The
Private Prayers of
POPE
JOHN PAUL II

The Loving Heart

Joannes Paulus II

The Private Prayers of Pope John Paul II

Words of Inspiration

An Invitation to Prayer

The Rosary Hour

The Loving Heart

Things To Do

(CARNITAS.)

- [ ] 896 0371
- [ ] Raul Diaz
- [ ]
- [ ]
- [ ]
- [ ]
- [ ]
- [ ]
- [ ]
- [ ]
- [ ]
- [ ]

The
Private Prayers of
POPE
JOHN PAUL II

The Loving Heart

ATRIA BOOKS

New York   London   Toronto   Sydney

ATRIA BOOKS
1230 Avenue of the Americas
New York, NY 10020

ISBN: 0-7434-4441-8

First Atria Books hardcover edition April 2005

10 9 8 7 6 5 4 3 2 1

ATRIA BOOKS is a trademark of Simon & Schuster, Inc.

Manufactured in the United States of America

For information regarding special discounts for bulk purchases,
please contact Simon & Schuster Special Sales at 1-800-456-6798 or
business@simonandschuster.com.

EDITOR'S NOTE

This edition is a translation of the work originally titled *Il Vangelo della Sofferenza* (The Gospel of Suffering), published in Italian in the Vatican City State. Like the previous books in this series, *Words of Inspiration, An Invitation to Prayer,* and *The Rosary Hour, The Loving Heart* retains the organization of the original.

CONTENTS

INTRODUCTION

"As the successor of Peter
I have to tell you
that the efficacy of my ministry
owes a great deal to the prayers
and offerings of the sick.
I confide this to you.
You occupy a large place
in my heart and in my prayers.
I count on you.
The Church counts on you."

Truly the sick and the world of suffering
have a special place
in the heart of John Paul II.
In audiences, on journeys,
during pastoral visits,
the encounters with those who suffer
are for him not only a duty
but also a source of inner comfort.
The teaching of John Paul II
on suffering is an encyclopedia!
The collection we present
will remind you of three truths:

1. The Church is a society where those who are suffering find a special welcome.
2. Christianity reveals that pain is not futile; rather, it conceals a true meaning and value.
3. Alongside those who suffer there is always a loving heart.

It is a heart capable of beating in tune with that of our brothers and sisters in pain.

Let us put the sick
at the center of our life.
Let us protect them
and gratefully recognize
the debt we owe them.
When we think of doing something for them,
we end by realizing
that it is we who are in their debt!

World Day of the Sick

Letter instituting the World Day of the Sick
A moment of prayer, sharing, and remembrance
To our reverend brother
Cardinal Fiorenzo Angelini, president of the Pontifical
    Council for Pastoral Assistance to Health Care
    Workers

Having favorably received the request from you, the above mentioned, as president of the Pontifical Council for Pastoral Assistance to Health Care Workers, and also as representative of various Episcopal Conferences and national and international Catholic organizations, I wish to tell you that I have decided to establish a World Day of the Sick, to be celebrated every year on February 11, the liturgical commemoration of the Blessed Virgin Mary of Lourdes. In fact, I consider it opportune to extend to the whole ecclesial community an initiative that, already in force in some countries and regions, has produced pastoral fruit that is truly precious.

The Church, which, following the example of Christ, has always recognized, throughout the centuries, the duty of service to the sick and the suffering as an integral part of its mission, is aware that "a fundamental motive of its mission today exists in giving a loving and generous welcome to every human life, above all those who are weak and sick."

Furthermore, the Church consistently emphasizes the salvific nature of the offering of suffering, which, lived in communion with Christ, belongs to the very essence of redemption.

The annual celebration of the World Day of the Sick therefore has the stated purpose of increasing the sensitivity of the People of God and, in consequence, of the many Catholic health-care facilities and of civil society itself to the need for insuring that the sick receive the best possible care; of helping those who are sick to value suffering, on the human and, above all, the supernatural level; of involving particularly the dioceses, the Christian communities, and religious Families in the health-care ministry; of remembering the importance of the spiritual and moral education of health-care workers; and, finally, of reminding both diocesan and regular priests, not to mention those who live and work with the sick, to understand the importance of religious help for the sick.

Just as on the date of February 11, 1984, I published the Apostolic Letter *Salvifici Doloris* on the Christian meaning of human suffering and, the following year, instituted this Pontifical Council for Pastoral Assistance to Health Care Workers, so I consider it meaningful to establish the same day for the celebration of the World Day of the Sick. In fact, "together with Mary, the Mother of Christ, who was at the Cross, let us stop at all the crosses of mankind today." And Lourdes, one of the most beloved Marian sanctuaries of the Christian people, is the place and at the same time the symbol of hope and grace in the sign of acceptance of suffering and of offering it for salvation.

4

I beg you, therefore, to bring to the attention of those in charge of the health-care ministry, in the bishops' conferences and in national and international organizations engaged in the vast network of health care, the institution of this World Day of the Sick, so that, in accord with local requirements and circumstances, its celebration may be properly carried out with the support of the entire People of God: priests, men and women religious, and lay faithful.

To that purpose, it will be the concern of this Dicastery to promote and encourage timely initiatives, so that the World Day of the Sick may be a special time of prayer and sharing, of offering one's suffering for the good of the Church, and of reminding everyone to see in his sick brother or sister the Holy Face of Christ, who, by suffering, dying, and rising, achieved the salvation of mankind.

While I hope for the full cooperation of all, so that this Day will have a strong start and rapid development, I entrust divine efficacy to the maternal mediation of Mary Salus Infirmorum, Health of the Sick, and to the intercession of the saints Giovanni di Dio and Camillo de Lellis, patrons of health-care workers and of institutions for the care of the sick. May these saints continue to increase the fruits of an apostolate of charity, which the modern world sorely needs.

May the Apostolic Blessing strengthen these vows, which I make to you from the depths of my heart, Signor Cardinal, and to those who help you in the work of serving the sick.

From the Vatican, May 13, 1992,

Ioannes Paulus II

Love for those who suffer is the sign and measure of the degree of civilization and progress of a people

The Christian community has always paid special attention to the sick and to the world of suffering in its many manifestations. In the wake of that long tradition, the universal Church, with a renewed spirit of service, is preparing to celebrate the first World Day of the Sick as a special occasion for growth, with an attitude of *listening, reflection,* and *effective commitment* in the face of the great mystery of pain and illness. That Day, which, beginning in February 1993, will be celebrated every year on February 11, the day of commemoration of Our Lady of Lourdes, seeks to be for all believers "a special time of prayer and sharing, of offering one's suffering for the good of the Church and of reminding everyone to see in his sick brother or sister the face of Christ, who, by suffering, dying, and rising, achieved the salvation of mankind."

The day seeks, further, to involve all people of goodwill. Indeed, the basic questions posed by the reality of suffering, in fact, and the appeal to bring both physical and spiritual relief do not concern only believers but challenge all humanity, marked by the limitations of the mortal condition.

Unfortunately, we are preparing to celebrate this first World Day in circumstances that are dramatic for several reasons: the events of these months, while bringing out the urgency of prayer in asking for help from on High, recall us to the duty of launching new and urgent initiatives of help for those who suffer and cannot wait.

Before the eyes of all are the sad images of individuals and whole peoples who, lacerated by war and conflicts, succumb under the weight of easily avoidable calamities. How can we turn our gaze from the imploring faces of so many human beings, especially children, reduced to a shell of their former selves by hardships of every kind in which they are caught up against their will because of selfishness and violence? And how can we forget all those who at health-care facilities — hospitals, clinics, leprosariums, centers for the disabled, nursing homes — or in their own dwellings undergo the calvary of sufferings that are often neglected, not always suitably relieved, and sometimes even made worse by a lack of adequate support?

Illness, which in everyday experience is perceived as a frustration of the natural life force, for believers becomes an appeal to "read" the new, difficult situation *in the perspective that is proper to faith.* Outside of faith, moreover, how can we discover in the moment of trial the constructive contribution of pain? How can we give meaning and value to the anguish, unease, and physical and psychic ills accompanying our mortal condition? What justification can we find for the decline of old age and the final goal of death, which, in spite of all scientific and technological progress, inexorably remain?

Yes, *only in Christ,* the incarnate Word, Redeemer of mankind and victor over death, *is it possible to find satisfactory answers to such fundamental questions.*

In the light of Christ's death and resurrection, illness no longer appears an exclusively negative event; rather, it is seen as a "visit by God," an opportunity "to release love, in order to give birth to works of love toward our neighbor, in order to transform the whole of human civilization into a civilization of love."

The history of the Church and of Christian spirituality offers very broad testimony of this. Over the centuries shining pages have been written of heroism in suffering accepted and offered in union with Christ. And no less marvelous pages have been traced out through humble service to the poor and the sick, in whose tormented flesh the presence of the poor, crucified Christ has been recognized.

The celebration of the World Day of the Sick—in its preparation, its unfolding, and its objectives—is not meant to be reduced to a mere external display centering on certain initiatives, however praiseworthy they may be, but is intended to reach consciences to make them aware of the valuable contribution that human and Christian service to those who suffer makes to better understanding among people and, consequently, to building real peace.

Indeed, peace presupposes, as its preliminary condition, that special attention be reserved for the suffering and the sick by public authorities, national and international organizations, and every person of goodwill. This is valid, first of all, for developing countries—in Latin America, Africa, and Asia—which are marked by serious deficiencies in health care. With the celebration of the World Day of the Sick, the Church is promoting a renewed commitment to those populations, and seeking to wipe out the injustice existing today by devoting greater human, spiritual, and material resources to their needs.

In this regard, I wish to address a special appeal to civil

authorities, to people of science, and to all those who work directly with the sick. May their service never become bureaucratic and impersonal! Particularly, may it be quite clear to all that the administration of public money imposes the serious duty of avoiding its waste and improper use so that available resources, administered wisely and equitably, will serve to insure prevention of disease and care during illness for all who need them.

The hopes that are so alive today for a humanization of medicine and health care require a more decisive response. To make health care more humane and adequate it is, however, essential to draw on a transcendent vision of man which stresses the value and sacredness of life in the sick person as the image and child of God. Illness and pain affect every human being: love for the suffering is the sign and measure of the degree of civilization and progress of a people.

To you, dear sick people all over the world, the main actors of this World Day, may this event bring the announcement of the living and comforting presence of the Lord. Your sufferings, accepted and borne with unshakable faith, take on, when joined to those of Christ, extraordinary value for the life of the Church and the good of humanity.

For you, health-care workers called to the highest, most meritorious, and exemplary testimony of justice and love, may this day be a renewed spur to continue in your delicate service, with generous openness to the profound values of the person, to respect for human dignity, and to the defense of life, from its beginning to its natural close.

For you, Pastors of the Christian people, and to all the different members of the Church community, for volunteers, and particularly for those engaged in the health-care ministry, may this World Day of the Sick offer stimulus and encouragement to go forward with fresh dedication on the path of service to tried, suffering humanity.

On the commemoration of Our Lady of Lourdes, whose shrine at the foot of the Pyrenees has become a temple of human suffering, we approach — as she did on Calvary, where the Cross of her Son rose up — the crosses of pain and solitude of so many brothers and sisters to bring them comfort, to share their suffering and present it to the Lord of life, in spiritual communion with the whole Church.

May the Blessed Virgin, Health of the Sick and Mother of the Living, be our support and our hope and, through the celebration of the Day of the Sick, increase our sensitivity and dedication to those being tested, along with the trusting expectation of the luminous day of our salvation, when every tear will be dried forever. May it be granted to us to enjoy the first fruits of that day from now on in the superabundant joy — though in the midst of all tribulations — promised by Christ which no one can take from us.

My blessing on all!

FROM THE VATICAN, OCTOBER 21, 1992
MESSAGE FOR FEBRUARY 11, 1993,
FIRST WORLD DAY OF THE SICK

The sick, the afflicted

It is these especially to whom,
at the very start of our pastoral ministry,
we wish to open our heart.
Is it not in fact you,
brothers and sisters,
who with your sufferings
share the passion of the Redeemer himself
and in some way complete it?
The unworthy successor of Peter,
who proposes to examine
the unfathomable riches of Christ,
sorely needs your help,
your prayer,
your sacrifice,
and for this reason
most humbly entreats you.

FIRST *URBI ET ORBI* MESSAGE,
OCTOBER 17, 1978

The Pope
in the Shadow
of the Cross

The incomparable effectiveness of suffering

Today I would like to address all sick people in a special way, as one who, like them, is ill, and offer a word of comfort and hope.

When, the day after my election to the throne of Peter, I visited the Gemelli Hospital, I said that I wished "to support my papal ministry above all on those who suffer."

Providence arranged that I should return to the Gemelli Hospital as a sick person myself. I will now reiterate the same conviction I held then: suffering, accepted in union with Christ who suffers, has an incomparable effectiveness in the realization of the divine plan of salvation. And here I will say again with St. Paul: "Now I rejoice in my sufferings for your sake, and in my flesh I complete what is lacking in Christ's afflictions for the sake of his body, that is, the Church."

I invite all sick people to join with me in offering their sufferings to Christ for the good of the Church and mankind. May Most Holy Mary sustain and comfort us.

AT THE GEMELLI HOSPITAL
AFTER THE ASSASSINATION ATTEMPT,
MAY 24, 1981

With me, offer your ordeal to the Lord

Dear ones, you who are sick, handicapped, or in frail health, and who are present at the Eucharistic Congress,

My affectionate thoughts and my prayers go out to all who have gathered at the grotto of Lourdes, but to you in a very special way.

Lourdes is the place where the sick, who come from all over the world, are always first, helped by their healthy brothers and sisters to offer their sufferings to the compassion of our Mother, the Virgin Mary, and to the mercy of Jesus Christ, and to leave with the comfort that comes from God.

You are closest to the heart of this Congress, which celebrates the real presence of Christ in the humble spoil of bread, the Christ who suffered and offered his Passion so that we might enter into Life and that his Kingdom might be opened to us.

You do not cease at any moment to be full members of the Church; not only, like others, are you in communion with the Body of the Lord but in your flesh you are in communion with the Passion of Christ. Your sufferings are not in vain: they contribute, invisibly, to the growth in Charity that animates the Church. The sacrament of Anointing of the Sick joins you in a special way to Christ, for the forgiveness of your sins, for the comfort of your body and soul, for the increasing hope of the Kingdom of Light and Life that Christ promises you.

Whenever I meet with the sick, in Rome or during my travels, I stop with each of them, I listen to them, I bless them, just as Jesus did, to show that each one is the object of God's tenderness.

At this moment God has allowed me to endure, in my own flesh, suffering and weakness. This makes me feel even closer to you, it helps me understand your ordeal even better. "Now I rejoice in my sufferings for your sake, and in my flesh I complete what is lacking in Christ's afflictions for the sake of his body, that is, the Church." I invite you to offer, together with me, your suffering to the Lord, who, through the Cross, achieves great things; to offer it so that the entire Church, through the Eucharist, may undergo a renewal of faith and charity; so that the world may know the benefit of forgiveness, of peace, of love.

May Our Lady of Lourdes sustain you in hope!

I bless all those who help you with their friendship and their care and who receive spiritual support from you.

And I bless you yourselves with all my affection, in the name of the Father and the Son and the Holy Spirit.

MESSAGE TO THE SICK ASSEMBLED AT
THE GROTTO OF LOURDES,
JULY 21, 1981

The "community" of the sick

Grateful as I am for the gift of life saved and health restored, I would like to express my gratitude for something more: that I have been granted the privilege, during these three months, to belong, dear brothers and sisters, to your community: to the community of the sick who are suffering in this hospital, and who for that reason constitute a special organism in the Church: in the mystical body of Christ. In a special way, according to St. Paul, one can say of them that they complete what is lacking in Christ's afflictions for the sake of his body. During these months I have had the privilege of belonging to this particular organism. And for that, too, I kindly thank you, brothers and sisters, at this moment, as I take my leave of you and your community.

Certainly there were and are among you many whose sufferings, incomparably greater than mine, and endured with love, bring you much closer to the Crucifixion and the Redeemer.

I have thought of this more than once, and so, as your Bishop, I have embraced all of you in my prayers. And sometimes I receive news of those whom the Lord of life has called to himself during these months.

All this, dear brothers and sisters, I have experienced daily, and I would like to tell you about it today, as I bid you farewell. Now I know better than ever before that *suffering* is one of those dimensions of life in which more than ever *the grace of redemption is grafted onto the human heart.*

And if I wish that each and every one of you may regain your health and leave this hospital, then with equal warmth I hope that you may take away from here the profound graft of divine life, which the grace of suffering carries with it.

AUGUST 14, 1981

Suffering asks us to be like Christ

I, too, have been assailed by suffering and have known the physical weakness that comes from disability and illness.

It is precisely because I have experienced suffering that I am able to repeat the words of St. Paul with even greater conviction: "Neither death, nor life, nor angels, nor principalities, nor things present, nor things to come, nor powers, nor height, nor depth, nor anything else in all creation, will be able to separate us from the love of God in Christ Jesus our Lord."

Dear friends, no force or power exists that can separate you from God's love. Illness and suffering seem contradictory to what is important for man and what man desires. And yet no malady, no weakness, no infirmity can deprive you of your dignity as children of God, as brothers and sisters of Jesus Christ.

By dying on the Cross, Christ reveals to us the meaning of our suffering. In his Passion we find the encouragement and strength to avoid every temptation to bitterness and, through pain, to grow into a new life. *Suffering is an invitation to be like the Son by doing the will of the Father.* We are offered the opportunity to imitate Christ, who died to redeem mankind from sin. Thus the Father wished suffering to enrich the individual and the whole Church.

UNITED KINGDOM,
MAY 28, 1982

I entrust to the Lord the sufferings of all sick people

Dearest brothers and sisters,

Today I am reciting the Angelus in a hospital, a place of suffering and hope, together with the doctors and the patients.

The expressions of solidarity that have come from all over the world have been a comfort to me.

Thank you! Thanks to the doctors and staff members of the Gemelli Hospital and the Vatican, who have been so attentive and so solicitous of me; thanks to those who in various ways have expressed their spiritual closeness with affectionate good wishes; thanks above all for the prayers, the most pleasing gift and the most effective means for getting through the harsh and painful moments of existence with faith and serenity.

Dearest brothers and sisters, I greet you and bless you all.

With the recitation of the Angelus, I entrust to the Lord, through the hands of Mary, the physical and spiritual sufferings of all the sick people in the world, together with my own, for the Church and for mankind.

RECITATION OF THE ANGELUS AT
THE GEMELLI HOSPITAL,
JULY 19, 1992

UNITED IN PRAYER AND AFFECTION
Give him back the joy of being able to shake the hands of the humblest in the world

O Lord,
yet again you wanted beside you, on the Cross,
our Pope John Paul II
to remind the world
that only on the Cross is resurrection and life.

Through the Cross you remind us that you
redeemed
the world. The disciple of Christ knows
that only if we embrace the Cross does the work
of Redemption
continue in time and in the history
of every man and every woman.

With the Pope a patient in the hospital, O Lord,
you let us
understand that he, too, crucified in the flesh,
is united with all those in the world who bear
stamped on them the stigmata of the Passion of
Jesus Christ.

Under the weight of the Cross the Pope,
following the example of Jesus, teaches us
to "love" the Cross. The Cross of the Christian
is always a Holy Cross:

teach us, O Lord, to learn to stay
under the sign of the Cross.

After the Cross, O Lord, comes the radiant dawn
of the Resurrection. Our Holy Father
already encountered this dawn of Resurrection
in May of 1981 after vanquishing the dark night
of that tragic event. As then, so today,
the Pope will return to serve the Church, having
once again loved it at the foot of the Cross.

O Lord, give John Paul II new strength
to serve the Church and all the peoples of the
    world.

Restore to him the joy of being able to shake
    the hands
of children, of orphans, of widows,
and of the humblest of the world.

For us the Holy Father is presence, is grace,
is hope, is certainty.

May our certainty, O Lord, not be damaged
in moments of suffering and hardship.
We thank you, O Lord, for all the good that you
    wish for us.

MOTHER TERESA OF CALCUTTA

I Count On You

I count on you

You know, dear brothers and sisters, how much I count on you, how much the Church counts on you. Meeting with you, in my ministry and my apostolic journeys, provides — I feel strongly — a sort of seal of authenticity, a guarantee of effectiveness, a mysterious and profound spiritual solidarity. I feel that in meeting with you I am following in the footsteps of the Savior of man. God speaks through suffering, opening new pathways, new horizons, and giving us the strength to complete those undertakings which the Lord suggests or commands.

Each of us, as I have said, has a particular task, a particular mission in this life. We can suffer for truth, we can suffer for justice, for peace, for the redemption of mankind. Suffering in Christ makes us children of God.

We constantly ask Christ the Teacher to enlighten us on the meaning of suffering. All of us have to learn from this mystery, which is apparently so abhorrent and yet — in Christ — is rich in spiritual values. St. Catherine of Siena said that the Cross is the school of all the virtues. Do we truly believe this? It is one of the great tasks of our present life: to reinforce, as firmly as possible, what Christ teaches us concerning the pain that saves. Knowing how to live justly here on earth depends on us. And on this depends our happiness in the present and in the future life.

Turin,
September 4, 1988

When, on October 17, 1978, the day after my unexpected elevation to the pontificate, I went to the Agostino Gemelli Hospital, I was not merely obeying a heartfelt impulse to visit some friends there, on Monte Mario. I also wished to give—and I can reaffirm it two years later—a precise idea of the way I conceived and conceive the formidable ministry of the successor of Peter. On that occasion I said to the patients that I counted on them; that, in fact, I counted on them a great deal. Through their prayers and, above all, through the offering of their sufferings I could derive a special power, which would enable me to fulfill in a worthier fashion my tremendous duties in the bosom of the Church of Christ. This very idea of an ecclesial communion, inspired and made more precious by the mysterious and yet very real contribution of those who suffer, I want to express to you again. I therefore repeat that *I count heavily on you,* and thank you for the help you bring, and I commend each of you to the Lord, who, as he is the master of life, so he is the master of mercy and consolation.

ROME, SAN GIACOMO HOSPITAL,
DECEMBER 21, 1980

You are my brothers and sisters in a special way

Dearest brothers and sisters,

I wish to greet from my heart all the sick, the bed-
ridden, and the handicapped in the name of the Lord
Jesus, who was himself "a man of sorrow and acquainted
with grief."

I would like to greet you one by one, bless you all
individually, and speak to you — to each of you individually — about Jesus Christ, who took on himself the suffering of mankind in order to bring salvation to the
whole world. God loves you as his honored children. You
are unique for two reasons: through the love of Christ
who unites us and, in particular, because you have a profound role in the mystery of the Cross and the redemption of Jesus.

Thank you for the sufferings that you endure in your
body and in your heart. Thank you for your example of
acceptance, patience, and union with Christ who suffers.
Thank you because "you complete what is lacking in
Christ's afflictions for the sake of his body."

May the peace and joy of the Lord Jesus be with you
always.

UNITED STATES,
OCTOBER 5, 1979

I count on the prayers of the sick

I count tremendously on the prayers of the sick, on their intercession with God. Those who suffer are so close to Christ! And I come to them knowing that Christ is present in them.

The suffering of our neighbor, the suffering of a man who is in every way like me, raises in those of us who do not suffer a certain unease, almost a sense of embarrassment. Instinctively a question arises: why him and not me? We cannot escape this question, which is the elementary expression of human solidarity.

Therefore we must pause when we are faced by his suffering, by the person who suffers, to rediscover this essential bond between my human "I" and his. We must stop before the person who suffers, to demonstrate to him and, as far as possible, with him, the dignity of suffering. We must bow our heads before our brothers or sisters who are weak and defenseless, deprived of the very thing which has been granted to us and which we enjoy every day.

Christ said, "I was sick and you visited me."

Let us pray for all the sick and for all who suffer, wherever they may be.

We are your debtors, dearest brothers and sisters who suffer. The Pope is your debtor.

Pray for us!

RECITATION OF THE ANGELUS,
FEBRUARY 11, 1979

Meeting with the old, the sick, and the handicapped always has a privileged place during my pastoral visits. You are not the forgotten children of God. On the contrary! Just as a sick child has a special place in the heart of its parents, so is God's joy in your faith and your courage that much greater. And Jesus Christ has assured us that it is in you that we meet him in a special way.

Unfortunately in the world of today not everyone realizes that those who are afflicted with old age, sickness, or a handicap have the same value as other human beings. And yet God is not interested in how productive we are or in the size of our bank account. The Lord looks not at appearances but at the heart.

God's loving gaze as it rests on each man and woman gives us the assurance that—old or young, healthy or sick—we are wanted or wished for, without exception. For this reason we all feel that we are sons and daughters of the same heavenly Father. God's love for us comes first and is fundamental. To experience this and to be conscious of it is truly something great; and it is important to participate in this experience with others and share it with them in life.

AUSTRIA,
JUNE 26, 1988

When people meet for the first time and wish to become friends, they usually introduce themselves. Do we need to do that? You already know my name and a lot about me. But, since I intend to become friends with you, I want to introduce myself: I come to you as a missionary sent by the Father and by Jesus to proclaim the Kingdom of God that begins in this world but is realized only in eternity; to consolidate the faith of my brothers and sisters; and to create a profound communion among all the children of the same Church. I come as the minister and unworthy vicar of Christ to watch over his Church; as the humble successor to the Apostle Peter, the Bishop of Rome and Pastor of the Universal Church.

Like Peter, I have agreed to be the universal Pastor of the Church, eager to know, love, and serve all the members of the flock entrusted to me. I am here to know you. My affection for all and each of you is vast. I am sure that in some way, at least, I will be able to serve you.

BRAZIL, LEPROSARIUM OF MARITUBA,
JULY 8, 1980

And you, who are you? For me you are first of all human beings, endowed with the immense dignity that is a condition of being a person, each one of you with the unique, unrepeatable personal features that God has given you. You are persons who have been saved by the blood of the One whom I like to call the "Redeemer of man," as I did in the first letter I wrote to the entire Church and the world. You are children of God, known and loved by him. You are and will be from now on and forever my friends, my very dear friends.

Therefore, blessed is God who grants us the grace of this meeting. It is indeed a grace for me, like the Lord Jesus whose minister and representative I am, to meet the poor and the sick, for whom he had a real preference. It is true that I cannot, like him, cure the ills of the body, but he will give me, through his goodness, the capacity to bring some comfort to hearts and souls. In this sense I hope that our meeting will be a grace for you, too. It is in the name of Jesus that we are here assembled: may he be among us as he promised.

Brazil, leprosarium of Marituba,
July 8, 1980

Why Suffering?

The mystery of pain

The mystery of pain tortures our existence. It isn't easy to accept pain and death, because it means accepting our frailty in its many dimensions. The mystery becomes even more profound when we enter into the suffering of Christ, the son of God, in whom all human pain finds its explanation and its transcendent meaning. Jesus, too, suffered pain and death, and he cried out, "My Father, if this cannot pass unless I drink it, thy will be done."

Moreover, if we can confront illness effectively, we can learn at the same time to discover God, to understand the pain of our fellow-men, and to be united with Christ, who suffers for mankind. This is to put into practice what St. Paul suggested: "In my flesh I complete what is lacking in Christ's afflictions for the sake of his body, that is, the Church."

BOLIVIA,
MAY 12, 1988

God wants to be close to every human being, but he is close to the sick with particular tenderness.

Yet human suffering leads us to doubt the words of Jesus that the Kingdom of God is near. When pain obscures the mind and weakens the body and soul, God may seem very far away, and life can become an intolerable burden. We are tempted not to believe in the Good News. Because, as the Book of Wisdom says, "A perishable body weighs down the soul, and this earthly tent burdens the thoughtful mind." The mystery of human suffering oppresses the sick person, and new and anxious questions arise:

> Why does God let me suffer?
> To what purpose?
> How can God, who is so good,
> allow so much evil?

There are no easy answers for the questions posed by the minds and hearts of the afflicted. But we cannot find a satisfactory response without the light of faith. We must call to God, our Father and Creator, as the author of the Book of Wisdom did:

> "With thee is wisdom, who knows thy works . . .
> Send her forth from the holy heavens . . .
> that she may be with me and toil, and
> that I may learn what is pleasing to thee."

NEW ZEALAND,
NOVEMBER 23, 1986

Suffering is an impenetrable mystery and so it is often difficult for us to understand, and to accept. The person who is afflicted by illness, or by any other sort of suffering, often wonders *Why must I endure this pain?* and almost immediately asks another question: *Why, what is the meaning of this suffering?* Not finding an answer, he is despondent, because the suffering becomes stronger than he is. Suffering is not a punishment for sins, nor is it God's response to man's evil. It can be understood only and exclusively in the light of God's love, which is the ultimate meaning of everything that exists in this world. Suffering "is linked to love"—as I wrote in the Apostolic Letter *Salvifici Doloris*—"to that love of which Christ spoke to Nicodemus, to that love which creates good, drawing it out by means of suffering, just as the supreme good of the redemption of the world was drawn from the Cross of Christ, and from that Cross constantly takes its beginning. In it we must also pose anew the question about the meaning of suffering, and read in it, to its very depths, the answer to this question."

In sickness, or in any other suffering, we must *abandon ourselves to the love of God,* like a child who entrusts everything he holds most dear to those who love him, especially his parents. Thus we need the capacity that children have to entrust ourselves to the One who is love.

POLAND,
JUNE 6, 1991

The good of redemption is concealed in suffering

Suffering is a great mystery in God's plan. Suffering is a great mystery of human destiny. To be sick or to have some bodily affliction is an experience that those who have never had have a hard time imagining: our body is wounded, but in the same way so is our spirit, our heart, our family and social life. And we question our spiritual life. Because suffering truly is *a mystery before God*. In fact, the man who suffers often asks God himself the question: Why? Why me? Why is there suffering on this earth?

There is no shortage of people who, in such a situation, are tempted to accuse God, to doubt, to turn away from him.

Dear friends, God the Father hears our "whys" and welcomes them, just as he heard Job's lament, as he heard the cry of anguish, the "why" of Jesus on the Cross as he trustfully surrenders. His answer is not what we would expect; it's not even the explanation that men have often given for suffering, seeing it as a punishment for their sins, or when, outside of rebelling, they could only resign themselves to it fatalistically. In the face of this mystery of suffering, the words of the prophet Isaiah acquire special eloquence: "For my thoughts are not your thoughts, neither are your ways my ways, says the LORD. For as the heavens are higher than the earth, so are my ways higher than your ways and my thoughts higher than your thoughts." These words can surely be applied *to the life of suffering*.

BELGIUM,
MAY 21, 1985

Only in suffering is true love possible

Why, O Lord, you who know everything and love everything, do you let such painful and disturbing things
happen?

Jesus himself gives us the answer, when he declares:
"Unless a grain of wheat falls into the earth and dies, it
remains alone; but if it dies, it bears much fruit." Jesus was
referring principally to his death on the Cross, for the redemption of mankind from sin, but the Christian has a
close association with this mystery: to produce the fruits
of goodness, of creation, of peace, we must pass through
detachment, suffering, and sometimes even death.

Genuine love is not possible except through suffering.

It is a superior, supernatural, divine logic, which is
always valid, but especially in spiritual life; if it upsets
our human plans, we must accept that with enlightened
faith and complete trust. Physical or moral suffering,
which comes upon us suddenly, is a call, an invitation, a
pressing exhortation to improve, to change our life, to be
reborn, to convert. Nothing happens by chance. In every
circumstance we must ask ourselves: "What does the
Lord want from me? From my situation, from this forced
inactivity, from the people I encounter—what is the
message that will enable me to purify my feelings, raise
my spirit, and hear the voice of truth and conscience?"

In this way an atmosphere and mutual bond of
friendship, familiarity, and kindness is formed, which
helps to overcome the stresses of illness and the possible
damage it does: then our ordeals do not frighten us or

make us bitter or angry, because charity is there, "which is patient and kind, isn't resentful, does not rejoice in wrong, bears all things, believes all things, hopes all things, endures all things."

"Lord, tell me the truth on your Cross"

In the eyes of the world, suffering, illness, and death are frightening, futile, and destructive. Especially when children have to suffer, when human beings who are innocent — and they are the majority — are stricken by illness, a handicap, or incurable pain, we find ourselves before an *enigma*, which we cannot honestly resolve by human means alone. It can make us cruel, it can embitter not only the one who is directly affected but also those who are close to him, and who, powerless to bring aid, suffer on account of that powerlessness.

Why? Why me? Why now? Why my wife, my father, my sister, my friend? These questions are understandable. On this earth no one can answer that "why." And yet the question "to what purpose" has this burden been placed on me can open up new horizons to us. When Jesus was asked if it was the blind man who sinned or his parents, he answered against every expectation: "It was not that this man sinned, or his parents, but that the works of God might be made manifest in him."

With this premise, the question "to what purpose" suggests an even more important word, which can provide the determining direction: "To what purpose, Lord?" This is no longer an insignificant question, which falls into the void, but, rather, is addressed to one who has suffered and has struggled to the last drop of blood, who "with loud cries and tears," as one reads in the Letter to the Hebrews, "learned obedience." He understands you and knows how you feel; he himself, at an early moment, prayed that the bitter cup be taken away. But he was so obedient to the will of the Father that in the end he could give his total and free assent. *From him you can learn to make your suffering rich in fruits and in meaning for the salvation of the world.* With him your illness and suffering can make you better men, and even happier and freer. Many have learned from him and so have been changed, by the source of comfort. Therefore go to the school of his suffering for our salvation and repeat the prayer that St. Catherine of Siena addressed to Christ during her many trials: "Lord, tell me the truth on your Cross, I want to listen to you."

As Christians, we see in illness not a grim or even senseless human destiny but, in the end, the mystery of the Cross and of the resurrection of Christ. In pain and suffering man shares the fate of creation, which—as St. Paul says—through sin has been "subjected to futility," which "has been groaning in travail," but which at the same time has already been animated by the hope that it "will be set free from its bondage to decay and obtain the glorious liberty of the children of God."

For a believer, illness and suffering are not a tragic fate that must be passively endured but, rather, a task, thanks to which he can live his Christian vocation in a special way. They are *the invocation of God to mankind:* an invocation to us to be fraternally close to those who are suffering and to help them using all the means offered by medical science; an invocation to the sick not to resign themselves to their suffering, or rebel out of bitterness, but, rather, to recognize in it *the possibility of a more intense form of following Christ.* Faith alone can give us courage and strength. If we are trustfully accepting, every human suffering can become personal participation in the offering of Christ who suffered for our sins in order to save the world. Thus the Passion of Christ continues in the individual who suffers. So, too, all the help and love we can manifest are in the end addressed to Christ. "I was sick and you visited me," Christ says, and continues, "Truly, I say to you, as you did it to one of the least of these my brethren, you did it to me."

Through the inner communion of suffering with Christ, human suffering receives a liberating and transforming power and by the same means *participates in the paschal hope* of future resurrection.

SWITZERLAND,
JUNE 16, 1984

Join your suffering to Christ's

Physical and moral suffering is undoubtedly one of the most moving mysteries of existence, for it touches each of us closely, excluding none. It is, by the law of nature, the daily bread of human beings, the permanent condition of life in every age.

Why do we suffer? That is the great question, to which many, having no answer, are unable to respond except by rebelling.

Well, faith inspired by the Gospel constitutes the answer that can satisfy the mind and fill the heart.

Only a life of faith sincerely accepted and intensely experienced can illuminate to its roots the mystery of suffering, alleviate it with the breath of hope, and, with the power of charity, even succeed in transforming it into joy and so into one of the levers that raise the world.

The Church, repeating the divine teaching, recalls that those who follow the footsteps of Jesus in tribulation are joined to his sufferings: they suffer with him to be glorified with him. And the Lord proclaims them blessed.

And so the mystery of human suffering, if it is accepted in the light of the mystery of Jesus and the Church, becomes an inexhaustible source of human and spiritual enrichment for all.

ROME, VILLA BETANIA HOSPITAL,
DECEMBER 19, 1982

The cross of your suffering is the source of grace

I know very well that, burdened by illness, we are tempted to lose heart. Frequently we ask ourselves in despair: Why this illness? What evil did I do to deserve it? A look at Jesus Christ in his earthly life and a look at faith, at the light of Jesus Christ, can change the way we think about our own situation. Christ the Son of God was innocent, yet he was acquainted with suffering in his own flesh. The Passion, the Cross — death on the Cross — were a cruel trial for him.

Your life is no different. Sickness truly is a cross, a cross that at times may be heavy, an ordeal that God allows in a person's life, in the unfathomable mystery of a plan that is beyond our capacity to comprehend. But suffering should not be looked at as blind fate. And it is not even necessarily or in itself a punishment. It is not something that destroys without leaving anything good. On the contrary, even when it is a burden for the body, the cross of illness carried in communion with the Cross of Christ becomes a source of salvation, of life or resurrection, for the sick person himself and for others, for all mankind.

I am sure that, seen in this light, illness, even if grievously painful, carries with it seeds of hope and inspiration for a new struggle.

BRAZIL,
JULY 8, 1980

47

Why?

Human suffering is a continent that none of us have reached the borders of: yet, traversing the pavilions of this "Little House," we have covered enough territory to get an idea of its impressive proportions. And the question again rises in our hearts: why?

In this unique environment, let's listen again to the response given by faith: the life of historical man, polluted by sin, unfolds under the sign of Christ's Cross. *In the Cross, God turned the meaning of suffering upside down*: suffering, which was the result and evidence of sin, has now become a sharing in the redemptive expiation brought about by Christ. As such, it carries in itself, even now, the anticipation of the ultimate victory over sin and its consequences, through sharing in the glorious resurrection of the Savior.

A few days ago, with the Liturgy leading us by the hand, we relived the dramatic moments of the Passion and death of the Lord, and we listened again to the triumphal Alleluia of the Resurrection. You see, the paschal mystery contains the ultimate word on human suffering: *Jesus assumes the pain of each of us in the mystery of his Passion and transforms it into a regenerative force* for those who suffer and for all mankind, with the prospect of the ultimate triumph of the resurrection, when "even so, through Jesus, God will bring with him those who have fallen asleep."

TURIN, COTTOLENGO,*
APRIL 13, 1980

---

*Piccola Casa della Divina Provvidenza, an institute dedicated to helping the sick, founded in 1832 by San Giuseppe Benedetto Cottolengo.

Jesus Christ: Suffering Vanquished by Love

Look at Christ crucified and learn from him!

We all know, through direct experience, that suffering and illness belong to the condition of man, who is a frail and limited creature, marked from birth by original sin. Frequently, those who are afflicted by illness yield to the temptation to consider it a divine "punishment," and as a result they doubt the goodwill of God, whom Jesus has revealed to us as the "Father" who *always* and *no matter what* loves his children.

In a society like ours, then, which claims to be built on well-being and consumerism, and which evaluates everything on the basis of efficiency and profit, the problems of illness and suffering, which cannot be denied, are "removed" or are considered to be solvable exclusively by means of advanced modern technology.

All of that constitutes a real "challenge" to those who profess to be believers, and who have in Revelation, and above all in the Gospel, an answer to welcome into their life and to offer to the world as a sign of hope and as the light that gives meaning to existence. It is the "word of the Cross," which all who work in the field of health care and sickness are called on to make their own, to attest to and proclaim to others.

You sick people, especially! The Pope, who has come among you today, says to you: *Look at Christ crucified and learn from him!*

Of course, illness and suffering remain a "limitation" and an "ordeal," and so they may constitute a stumbling block on the road of life. In the perspective of the Cross, however, they become *a moment of increased faith* and a valuable instrument by means of which, joined with Christ, we contribute to the realization of the divine plan of salvation.

Dearest brothers and sisters who are sick, this is how you must experience your suffering.

ROME, FIGLIE DI SAN CAMILLO HOSPITAL,
APRIL 1, 1990

Pain finds comfort only in Christ

I ask you to become more and more aware of the mission that the Lord has entrusted to you. Do you know that Christ calls you, as privileged brothers and sisters, to take part in his work? It's hard to understand this, and even harder to accept it. But surely it's an ideal you would like to achieve.

All those for whom suffering is a tragic enigma that seems to have no possible satisfactory solution will find comfort in the example of Jesus, who approached the world of human suffering and is unfailingly beside it, taking it upon himself. He, the Innocent One, illuminates the mystery of suffering through love, which makes pain effective in the work of salvation. In him, God made of suffering and dying an instrument of redemption, the door through which we may obtain the life without end.

May the grace of God open your hearts, so that you may know and understand the deep love of He who is light and life for all men.

Know that God loves you and is near you. He is fully aware of your tribulations and also your aspirations. May faith in him always be light and comfort to you.

I entrust you to the Virgin Mary. Maintain a constant, spontaneous devotion to this gentle, caring mother. Turn to God, along with her, for your material and spiritual needs. Turn to her, praying to her for the Church: that the Lord may always have his rightful place on this earth; that every human being may be respected and loved, understood and helped.

RAVENNA, MAY 11, 1986

53

Trust in Christ's great love

I invite you to trust in Christ's great love for those who suffer. God loves the poor and the sick and, while man may be tempted to consider that the only life worth living is one that is productive, that transforms the world, that is effective, he instructs us through his Son to love those who suffer; and he helps us to observe that it is in suffering that man shows himself to be far more capable of expressing the human values of the spirit, such as friendship, affection, love — all those qualities, that is, which in suffering and need are much more exalted and more profoundly comprehended. I would therefore like to ask you to consider the moments of your suffering as a mysterious vocation. "Suffering is a call to demonstrate the moral greatness of man, his spiritual maturity"; but it is also a call from Providence to draw closer to the Crucified One, to understand him, to share his mystery. Feel that with your crosses you are close to God, and with Christ offer them to God the Father, so that the real contribution of your sacrifice generates precious moments of grace for humanity and for the Church. By meditating on the Passion of Christ you will find the strength to transform the momentary weight of illness into a holy offering.

MARCH 16, 1986

God loves you in a special way, and is particularly close to you

During his earthly life, Jesus was particularly close to those who were suffering.

He loved the sick. What people call misfortunes Jesus called blessings. He did this because *by redeeming our suffering he gave it immense value,* which only the heart of a believer can know.

The Gospel of suffering is necessary especially for you who live here: you who are afflicted by leprosy. You need to know that *Christ is particularly close to you.* In this Gospel of suffering we find praise for those who have persevered through the ordeals imposed by suffering.

To the unspeakable anguish of the question "Why me?" Jesus offers the vivid response of his death on the Cross, since he suffered exclusively for others, offering himself with endless love. And from that time we, too, "have always carried in our body the death of Jesus, so that Jesus' life may manifest itself in our body." In this way we can understand how Christ's suffering — his death and resurrection, his saving act of love — is truly the source of dignity for all suffering, just like the promise of future glory that is about to be revealed to us.

KOREA, SOROKDO LEPROSARIUM,
MAY 4, 1984

Christ gives meaning to our pain

Of course I could not forget you, who among the limbs of Christ's body, which is the Church, are most deserving of care and attention.

I have come here to assure you of my active participation in your sufferings. Know that the Pope is near you with special affection and, above all, that he prays for you, so that the Lord may ease your pain and, even more, allow you to face it with inner strength and an evangelical spirit.

When we Christians have the experience of pain, we must be careful to give it its proper meaning. It is not a punishment but an occasion for purifying our sins. In particular, it has as its end the good of men and women, our brothers and sisters: as it did for Jesus, who gave himself for the Redemption of us all. Therefore, through faith, join your tribulations to those endured by him. We must carry our crosses in his footsteps, otherwise they become too heavy. But with Jesus Christ ahead of us, we walk more quickly, for he gives meaning and direction to all our sufferings.

And receive my most heartfelt wishes for a speedy and total recovery, according to the will of God.

SIENA,
SEPTEMBER 14, 1980

Dearest brothers and sisters, take heart! You have an exalted task to perform: you are called to "complete in your flesh what is lacking in Christ's afflictions for the sake of his body, that is, the Church." With your pain you can fortify wavering souls, recall to the straight path those who have deviated, restore serenity and trust to those who are filled with doubts and anguish. Your sufferings, if generously accepted and offered together with those of the Crucified One, can make an outstanding contribution in the struggle for the victory of good over the forces of evil, which threaten mankind today in so many ways.

> In you Christ extends
> His redeeming Passion.
> With him, if you want,
> you can save the world!

TURIN, COTTOLENGO,
APRIL 13, 1980

Christ is our traveling companion

Christ is with us: this certainty spreads immense peace and profound joy in our hearts. We know we can count on him here and everywhere, now and forever. He is the friend who understands us and supports us in our dark moments, because he is the "man of sorrows who is acquainted with grief." He is the traveling companion who restores warmth to our hearts, enlightening us with the treasures of wisdom contained in the Scriptures. He is the living bread that came down from Heaven, who can light in our mortal flesh the spark of the life that does not die.

Let us therefore resume our journey with renewed energy. The Holy Virgin shows us the way. Like the luminous morning star, she shines before the eyes of our faith, "that sign of sure hope and consolation, until the day of the Lord shall arrive." Pilgrims in this "vale of tears," we sigh to her: "After this our exile show unto us the blessed fruit of your womb, Jesus, O clement, O loving, O sweet Virgin Mary!"

FEBRUARY 11, 1980

The Church
and
Those Who Suffer

It is well known that the Church has always taken a deep interest in the world of the suffering. And yet in this it has merely followed the eloquent example of its Founder and Master. In the Apostolic Letter *Salvifici Doloris* of February 11, 1984, I emphasized that "in his messianic activity in the midst of Israel, Christ drew increasingly closer *to the world of human suffering.* 'He went about doing good,' and his actions concerned primarily those who were suffering and seeking help."

In fact, in the course of the centuries the Church has felt strongly that service to the sick and suffering is an integral part of its mission, and it has not only encouraged among Christians the flowering of various works of mercy but also established many religious institutions within itself with the specific aim of fostering, organizing, improving, and increasing help to the sick. Missionaries, for their part, in carrying out the work of evangelization, have constantly combined the preaching of the Good News with the help and care of the sick.

MOTU PROPRIO DOLENTIUM HOMINUM,
FEBRUARY 1-11, 1985

The Church is not indifferent

In every age, the institutions of society charged with watching over public health are called on to undertake every possible effort to insure that the population is protected; but this cannot be done except in regard to every person and the whole person — that is, both by preventing the spread of the illness and by taking care of those who have been afflicted. The degree of civility of a society can be measured by the manner in which it responds to the exigencies of life and the sufferings of its members, for the frailty of the human condition means that solidarity is required in order to safeguard the sacred character of life, from its beginning to its natural end, in each moment and in every phase of its evolution.

The Catholic Church, which received from its founder, Jesus Christ, the inheritance of a special and caring relationship with those who suffer — an inheritance that it has had from the beginning — certainly is not indifferent to the fate of this new category of sick people. They, too, must be considered brothers and sisters, whose human condition calls for a special form of solidarity and help.

MESSAGE FOR WORLD AIDS DAY,
DECEMBER 1, 1988

Never, in the course of centuries, has the Church lost sight of the insistent admonition of the Lord to visit the sick, as a fundamental principle of its identity: a visit to the sick is equivalent to an homage made to the Lord himself.

Jesus, who suffered himself, and in fact freely chose the most terrible suffering, out of love for us, always looked upon the sick with special love: he approached them so that he could heal them in body and spirit, and they, as if by instinct, went to meet him as soon as they saw him. From then on, saints and true Christians followed his example, and the Church, never tired of urging the faithful to go in that direction, has been for two thousand years the inspiration for works and religious congregations devoted exclusively to the service of the sick.

Enlightened by the divine word of Jesus, the Church is aware that it is suffering, together with prayer, that saves the world. And, while it encourages medical science to find new and more efficacious treatments for the ills of the body, it invites the sick not to waste the occasion of suffering but to offer it to God as a sacrifice of purification and a gift of salvation.

TREVISO,
JUNE 16, 1985

It is in you above all, brothers and sisters in Jesus Christ, that the Church sees the source and the most effective instruments of the divine force that is concealed in it. In fact, by looking at you, who share in Christ's sufferings, the Church will understand if you can keep alive hope, which gives meaning to suffering endured in love; if you, as joyous Christians, can bear witness to your faith, as you follow in the footsteps of Mary, who traveled her road with simplicity, and was constantly available to God and men; if in the course of your life you can bear witness to that which is transient and that which belongs to eternity, distinguishing between the superficial and the essential.

The man inspired by the Holy Spirit must listen to others, console, encourage, and take responsibility, establish peace and inspire new hope. The fruit of the spirit is love, joy, peace, patience, kindness, goodness, gentleness, and self-possession. The place where the fruit matures carries the seed of eternal spring. May the Lord open your hearts so that you may understand these things.

The Spirit of the Lord wishes to console and comfort you, too, as once he accompanied and inspired the apostles and St. Paul in the difficulties and challenges of their ministry.

"Behold, I stand at the door and knock," says the Lord. "If any one hears my voice and opens the door, I will come in to him and eat with him, and he with me."

Open the doors of your hearts to the Lord, for you, too, must be witnesses of his presence and of the comfort he brings!

May the Virgin Mary accompany you and sustain you with her maternal protection.

HOLLAND, MAY 13, 1985

66

You have an important role to play in the Church

In the *Church* you have an important role to play. You are called to participate fully in its life and in its *mission in the world*.

Each of you, through baptism, enjoys the gift of a new life in Christ and the dignity of being an adopted son or daughter of our Father in Heaven. Through Baptism you have participated in *the priestly, prophetic, and royal offices of our Lord Jesus Christ;* and you are called to carry out your mission, whose purpose is to form the body of Christ, the Church, and promote the Kingdom of God in this world. Your personal call to sanctity and to the service of love for your neighbor is not separated from your daily life. Rather, your patient endurance of infirmity and your joyous hope in the face of adversity are in their way a proclamation of the Gospel, because they carry silent testimony of the salvific power of God who operates in your lives.

"Therefore be imitators of God, as beloved children," St. Paul said. "And walk in love, as Christ loved us." Try to accept every eventuality with the spirit of faith and in the light of the Cross. And may you find in the Eucharist and in prayer the strength needed to overcome every obstacle, and the liberating power of Christ who has conquered the world.

Dear brothers and sisters in Christ: be assured that you are not alone. The Lord loves you and has given you a special place in the Church. The Pope loves you and blesses you with all his heart. And he invites you to be near him every day when he celebrates the holy Eucharist and when he says the Holy Mass, offering Christ himself as the victim of the entire world. Your place is beside suffering and crucified Christ in the triumph of the Eucharist. The Pope is near your families, too, and all those who are dear to you. May Christ fill you with his peace.

CANADA,
SEPTEMBER 12, 1984

You collaborate with Christ in the work of salvation

The Church, like Jesus, its Redeemer, wants *to always be near those who suffer*. It raises them to the Lord with prayer. It offers them consolation and hope. It helps them find meaning in fear and in pain, teaching them that suffering is not a divine punishment or a consequence of evildoing by malignant spirits. The Church holds up Christ as an example, who, through his Crucifixion and Resurrection, redeemed all the suffering of mankind and so gave meaning to this mystery of human existence.

Dear brothers and sisters, I want you to know how important you are for the Church, because you play an irreplaceable role in its mission of salvation. Joining your sufferings to the sacrifice of Christ, *you help others to share in the redemption of Christ*.

In seeking to experience the mystery of suffering in union with Christ, be men and women of prayer. St. James says: "Pray for one another, that you may be healed. The prayer of a righteous man has great power in its effects." Try especially to encourage and sustain your brothers and sisters who suffer. Let your suffering, endured in the love of Christ, fill your heart with compassion and pity.

May our heavenly Father "supply every need of yours according to his riches in glory in Christ Jesus." And may the love of Jesus be always in your hearts.

PAPUA NEW GUINEA,
MAY 8, 1984

You are in the heart of the Church

I am sure that you have often pondered the meaning and the value of your suffering. With you in mind, I wrote an Apostolic Letter on the Christian meaning of human suffering. I wished to declare to the world that "in suffering there is concealed a particular power that draws a person inwardly close to Christ, a special grace."

This closeness to Christ who suffers places you in the very heart of the Church on its pilgrimage toward the Kingdom of God. And since you are in the heart of the Church you are also in my heart. I ask you to pray for the Church and to intercede for the whole family of man in these times of great need.

I assure you that I remember you in my daily prayers and I ask the Virgin Mother of our Redeemer to be always with you.

APRIL 5, 1984

70

Like Jesus, the Church is close to those who suffer in body and spirit. Just as it was yesterday, during a two-thousand-year history, which inspired in great and holy souls various creative forms of assistance, according to the needs of the moment, so it is still today, in every part of the world, in spite of the changed conditions of the times and the fact that the political authorities have assumed a more direct role in the area of religion.

The Church wants to be near those who suffer because it considers them brothers and sisters who are objects of special attention on the part of the divine Teacher.

Jesus was eager to be with the sick. They knew him, and so they turned to him. He was interested in their personal situation, in their needs, he listened to the story of their sufferings, he cured them of illness, at times even by the extraordinary means of a miracle; and he never tired of admonishing his disciples to visit the sick as an indispensable condition of reaching the kingdom of the Father.

The Church considers its activity on behalf of the sick to be a mark of love. Just as from its origins the Church was united around the Eucharistic Supper, so, in every age, it can be seen in the multiple forms of charity, through which it manifests its maternal love.

For this reason the Church claims works of charity as its duty and its inalienable right; and for the same reason, while it charges the State to intervene in the field of health, it is also eager to endorse the principle of subsidies, in order to exclude any form of monopoly. Helping one's neighbor is a right and a duty for all.

ROME, VILLA BETANIA,
DECEMBER 19, 1982

71

Your sufferings enrich the Church

Dear sick people, you occupy a special place in my heart, because, although you are physically weak and poor, you enrich the Church with your sufferings, borne in union with Crucified Christ. In saying this I know I am stating the central mystery of Christianity: the "incredible" mystery of the Son of God who, to save us, assumed the condition of a servant, becoming like us and making himself obedient until death and death on the Cross.

You sick people take part in this mystery in a very special way, sharing with Christ the weight of the Cross, whose hard wood you feel pressing into your flesh, which is afflicted by illness. But you also know that, for this very reason, you have a privileged role in the building of the Church, making an irreplaceable contribution to its expansion and purification.

> I count on your spiritual support:
> your suffering is my strength,
> because in your suffering
> the redeeming force of Christ's Cross is at work.

Be near me with the offer of your prayers and your sacrifices! From this moment I thank you, and I hold you all close to my heart in a vast embrace.

My appreciation and respect go equally to those who help you with loving and tireless care. I hope that consciousness of their noble mission in the service of life is ever more alive in their spirits. May they feel more and more every day how beautiful it is to devote their existence to the service of human life; and how praiseworthy to give health, a smile, and joy in life to so many brothers and sisters.

May the Lord help you in this work, dear ones, and give you the courage to be faithful to those moral principles that make the medical profession sacred.

BRESCIA,
SEPTEMBER 26, 1982

The Church with those who suffer

Today people suffer.

How much, how much suffering there is in the world when we forget that men and women are our brothers and sisters! Well, the Church, in looking at the mystery of the Son of God made man — and, because of the injustice of men, he, too, was exposed to suffering and hunger, poverty, exile — the Church cannot help intervening, taking responsibility, getting involved in helping people, to spare them from suffering.

> Wherever someone is suffering,
> there is Christ waiting alongside him.
> Wherever someone is suffering,
> the Church must be there at his side.

DECEMBER 22, 1979

The Church prays for the health of all the sick, of all who suffer, of all who are incurable, condemned to be permanent invalids. It prays *for* the sick and *with* the sick. It is tremendously grateful for every recovery, even if it is partial and gradual. And at the same time, its whole attitude leads us to understand—like Christ—that recovery is something exceptional, that from the point of view of the divine "economy" of salvation it is a marvelous fact, like something "extra."

FEBRUARY 11, 1979

Offer your suffering for the benefit of the Church

I pray that you may not be discouraged or bitter. Wherever and whenever you meet the Cross, embrace it as Jesus did, so that the will of the Father may be done. May your suffering be offered for the benefit of the whole Church.

Share the convictions of your faith with your brothers and sisters who suffer with you. Return the love of the doctors, nurses, and volunteers who so generously take care of you. Work to construct a community of living faith, a community that gives support, that strengthens and enriches the universal Church.

> Here is your service to Christ!
> Here is the challenge for your life!
> It is here that you can manifest your faith,
> your hope, and your love!
>
> PHILIPPINES, TALA LEPROSARIUM,
> FEBRUARY 21, 1981

I exhort you to a more and more *intense*
and profound love for the Church,
which always, but especially today,
must be entirely united in truth,
in charity, and in discipline.
You sick people, too,
who see how mankind
is confused and threatened,
searching for certainty and truth,
take part in this mysterious passion
in a special way:
pray, then, and suffer for the Church,
for the bishops and the priests,
for vocations, for the seminaries,
and for those in charge of
priestly and religious formation.
The Church needs
people who pray and love
in silence and in suffering:
and you, truly,
in your illness,
can be those apostles!

FEBRUARY 11, 1984

I feel that I am an active participant in your life, which is marked by suffering, but loved in a special way by the Lord, who — as the Gospels tell us — is particularly close to those who are most severely tested by suffering.

You, with your prayers and with the testimony of kindness, can offer a daily contribution to the cause of bringing peace to our hearts and peace among men. I have come to tell you that the Pope counts on your hidden but effective support: ask God for the gift of peace in our hearts, in families, among peoples.

Dearest ones! Prayers may seem ineffectual and vain in the face of the tragedies of men, and yet they open up new windows of hope, especially when they are strengthened by suffering that is transformed into love.

ASSISI,
JANUARY 9, 1993

The Gospel of Suffering

The Gospel often shows Jesus in the act of bending over sick people, to comfort them and also, not infrequently, to cure them.

The Redeemer himself did not escape suffering, and he taught that pain has a value in the work of salvation, yet "he went about doing good and healing all." A double lesson can be seen in this behavior: that human *pain* has a precise role to play in God's plan, and that, nevertheless, it *moves the heart of Jesus to compassion,* for he knows well how profoundly suffering can upset frail humanity and how severely it can test it. Thus he never withholds his understanding and comfort from the sick person who turns trustingly to him.

It is very important, in fact crucial, *to accept suffering with Jesus, like Jesus, and for his love,* because this conforms in a special way with him and his mission. In this regard St. Maximus the Confessor teaches that God, in his inscrutable plan of love, allows suffering to strike mankind not only as a punishment but as a medicine.

The plea to be cured is still legitimate, because health, too, is a great gift of God, thanks to which we may render valuable services to our neighbor. No divine gift, in fact, is ever bestowed for our exclusive personal advantage but "so that we may be able to comfort those who are in any affliction, with the comfort with which we ourselves are comforted by God."

FIDENZA,
JUNE 4, 1988

81

Suffering is a cause for joy, not sorrow

The Pope wished to come among you to tell you that Christ, who is always close to those who suffer, calls you to him. Even more: to tell you that you are called to be "other Christs" and to take part in his mission of redemption. And what is holiness if not to imitate Christ, and identify with him? Those who approach suffering with a purely human vision cannot understand its meaning and can easily fall into despair; at most, they may reach a point of accepting it with a melancholy resignation to the inevitable. We Christians, on the other hand, instructed in faith, know that suffering—if we offer it to God—can transform us into an instrument of salvation and put us on a pathway to sanctity, which leads us to Heaven. For a Christian, suffering is a cause not for sorrow but for joy: the joy of knowing that on the Cross of Christ every one of our sufferings has a redeeming value.

Today, too, the Lord calls us saying: "Come unto me, who labor and are heavy laden, and I will give you rest." Therefore, turn your gaze to him, in the sure hope that he will give you relief, that in him you will find consolation. Do not be afraid to show him your sufferings, and sometimes even your solitude; offer him this together with your daily crosses, large and small, and so—even if they frequently seem to you unbearable—they will not weigh you down, because it is Christ himself who will carry them for you: "Surely he has borne our griefs and carried our sorrows."

Following Christ on this path, you will feel the inner joy of doing God's will. It is a joy that is compatible with sorrow, because it is the joy of the children of God, who know they are called to follow Jesus more nearly on the road to Golgotha.

ARGENTINA,
APRIL 8, 1987

The Gospel gives meaning to our sufferings

To talk to you about joy, dear sick people, may seem strange and contradictory; and yet precisely in this is the overwhelming value of the Christian message. Jesus, carrying the light of Truth through Revelation and salvation from sin through Redemption, has given mankind the treasure of true joy: "This is my commandment, that you love one another as I have loved you." "No one will take your joy from you. . . . Ask, and you will receive, that your joy may be full." It is an inner joy, mysterious, sometimes even marked by tears, but it is always alive, because it originates in the assurance of the love of God, who is always the Father — even in the painful and adverse circumstances of life — and in the certainty of the high and eternal value of all human existence, especially when it is tormented by suffering and deprived of human satisfactions.

"Christ did not abolish suffering," the fathers of Vatican II said in their message to the poor and the sick, "and was unwilling to unveil the mystery entirely; he took it on himself and that is sufficient for us to understand its full value." This is the only truth that can respond to our questions and bring us comfort without illusions.

ON THE 80TH ANNIVERSARY OF
THE FOUNDING OF UNITALSI,*
FEBRUARY 11, 1983

---

*Unitalsi, or Unione Nazionale Italiana per Trasporto Ammalati Lourdes e Santuari Internazionali, is an organization that helps the sick travel to Lourdes and other international sanctuaries.

Dearest brothers and sisters who suffer in body and soul, know that the Church places its trust in you, and the Pope counts on you, so that the name of Jesus may be proclaimed to the ends of the earth. I would also like to remind you of what I wrote in the letter on the Christian meaning of human suffering: "The Gospel of suffering is being written unceasingly, and it speaks unceasingly with the words of this strange paradox: the springs of divine power gush forth precisely in the midst of human weakness. Those who share in the sufferings of Christ preserve in their own sufferings a very special particle of the infinite treasure of the world's redemption, and can share this treasure with others. The more a person is threatened by sin, the heavier the structures of sin that today's world brings with it, the greater is the eloquence that human suffering possesses in itself. And the more the Church feels the need to have recourse to the value of human sufferings for the salvation of the world."

May Mary, Queen of Martyrs, and Queen of the Apostles, awaken in all of you the desire to be joined to the passion of Christ the universal redeemer.

JUNE 10, 1984

Suffering makes us precious collaborators with Christ

Suffering is always a reality, a reality with a thousand faces. There are so many illnesses and infirmities: some curable with time, others unfortunately incurable. Suffering is certainly objective; but it is even more subjective, unique in the sense that ill or afflicted persons, faced with the same malady, react differently, sometimes very differently. It is the mystery of each person's sensibility, which is imponderable.

Healthy people who are confronted by suffering have a primary duty: respect, which can sometimes take the form of silence. In spite of partial explanations, suffering remains difficult to understand and difficult to accept even for those who have faith. Faith, in fact, does not eliminate our suffering. It joins it invisibly to that of Christ the Redeemer, the spotless Lamb, who is as if immersed in the sin and misery of the world, in order to be in total solidarity with us, and to give suffering another meaning, sanctifying in advance all the ordeals, including death itself, that men and women his brothers and sisters must endure in body and soul. "Through Christ and in Christ, the riddles of sorrow and death grow meaningful. Apart from His Gospel, they overwhelm us." This statement is cited in the marvelous *Constitution on the Church in the Contemporary World*.

LOURDES,
AUGUST 15, 1983

The Cross of Christ gives meaning to your suffering

At this moment I wish I had thousands of hands so that I could reach out and shake the hand of each one of you, to ask how you are, to share at least for a moment your anxieties and sufferings, and leave you with a word of encouragement and a fraternal embrace.

You who live amid tribulations, who are faced with the problem of limitations, of suffering and inner solitude, *do not cease to give meaning to this condition*. The answer lies in the Cross of Christ, in the redemptive union with him, in the apparent failure of the just Man who suffers yet who with his sacrifice saves mankind, with the eternal value of this suffering. Look at him, at the Church, and at the world, and raise up your suffering, completing with it, today, the mystery of his Cross that brings salvation.

Your suffering has a great supernatural importance. And, besides, you are a constant example, inviting us to evaluate so many principles and forms of life, in order to live the values of the Gospel better, and to develop solidarity, kindness, help, love.

Therefore, do not consider your condition worthless; for the Church and for the world of today it has immense meaning, in that it humanizes, evangelizes, atones, and prays for us.

SPAIN,
NOVEMBER 6, 1982

May your suffering become redeeming love

At this moment I would like to express the deep sympathy that I feel for each of you, and all my understanding for the sickness you carry in your body and your spirit; I would like to speak with you one by one to instill in you comfort and encouragement.

Your life as handicapped persons constitutes a great trial; it is a trial for you above all, but also for your parents, for those who love you, and for those who wonder: why this infirmity?

In fact, your ordeal is also a mystery.

The Lord does not ask us to close our eyes in the face of infirmity. It is very real, and we must have a clear knowledge of it. He asks us to look more deeply, to believe that in these suffering bodies beats not only human life with all its dignity and its rights but also, by virtue of baptism, the divine life, the marvelous life of the children of God. If to the external eyes of men you appear weak and infirm, before God you are great and luminous in your existence.

There is yet another important reality that Jesus reveals to us.

In human society, powerful, cultivated people occupy the positions of authority and are more visible; in the Kingdom of God, on the other hand, the opposite happens — the first and the greatest, Jesus tells us, are the children, the weak, the poor, the suffering. The ways of God are disturbing to mankind. St. Paul says: "God chose what is weak in the world to shame the strong."

This truth, which leaves us bewildered, becomes comprehensible if we look at the example of Jesus. Jesus was not content with revealing to us the mystery of suffering. He gave us the most convincing answer by taking our weaknesses upon himself, becoming the Man of sorrow who is acquainted with suffering.

When we ask God, then: Why must this innocent suffer? God, in turn, asks us a question: Do you not see me in your brother who suffers? And what will you do for me and for him?

ROME, INSTITUTE DON GUANELLA,
MARCH 28, 1982

Give me your sufferings,
Brothers and sisters!
I will bring them to the altar,
to offer them to God the Father,
in communion with those
of his only begotten Son,
and to pray,
in their name,
for peace for the Church,
mutual understanding among nations,
the humility of repentance for those who
    have sinned,
the generosity of forgiveness
for those who have been injured —
for all the joy
of a renewed experience
of the merciful love of God.
May the Most Holy Virgin,
who was "standing by the Cross of Jesus"
when he died for us,
rouse in our hearts
feelings suitable
for this hour of light and grace.
Amen.

SANCTUARY OF COLLEVALENZA,
NOVEMBER 22, 1981

In the following of our Lord who suffers

The Pope wishes to show you, dear handicapped brothers and sisters, his deep affection and respect for you, and the great trust that he places in you and in your help through prayer and the offering of your affliction — and above all through patient and generous acceptance of your suffering.

Look at your fate with the eyes of faith. What seems a tragic misfortune to those who do not believe can become for believers a task that is highly charged with meaning and that can bring fulfillment to life in human society and in the Church. In the destiny allotted to us not by blind chance but by a merciful God, and accepted as such, his call comes to meet us personally. In it we recognize the vocation and the task that have been entrusted to us. As you stand before the Cross, try to understand your vocation more and more profoundly, a vocation that is inseparable from your physical handicap, and try to welcome it with an increasing inner readiness for the following of Christ who suffers, and make it productive for the activity of the Church.

Share in the Eucharist, and every day join your ordeal and your sufferings anew to the redemptive suffering of Jesus Christ, in which your illness acquires an inestimable value in the eyes of God and his providential plan of salvation.

SEPTEMBER 29, 1981

91

To the victims of AIDS

I address myself above all, with heartfelt solicitude, *to those who are afflicted with AIDS*.

Brothers in Christ, who know all the bitterness of the way of the Cross, be assured that you are not alone. *The Church* is with you, with the sacrament of salvation, to sustain you on your difficult road. The Church receives a great deal from your suffering, if it is confronted in faith; the Church is beside you with the comfort of the active solidarity of its members, so that you will never lose hope. Do not forget the call of Jesus: "Come unto me, who labor and are heavy laden, and I will give you rest."

With you, dearest ones, are *men of science,* who work tirelessly to contain and defeat this grave illness; with you are many who, as health professionals or as volunteers, sustained by the ideal of human solidarity, will attend to you with devoted care and every means available.

You, in turn, can offer something significant to the community that you belong to. The effort that you make to give meaning to your suffering is a precious reminder to all of the highest values of life and a perhaps decisive support for those who are tempted by desperation. Do not be shut up in yourselves, but try and accept the help of your brothers and sisters.

The Church raises up prayers to the Lord for you every day, and especially for those of you who suffer your illness in abandonment, in solitude; for orphans, for the weakest, for the poorest, whom the Lord has taught us to consider the first in his kingdom.

AT THE INTERNATIONAL CONGRESS ON AIDS,
NOVEMBER 15, 1989

You are precious in the eyes of the Lord

When I think of you, the words uttered by the Lord through the prophet Isaiah come to mind: "because you are precious in my eyes, because you are worthy of esteem and I love you." You are truly *precious in the eyes of the Lord* and in the eyes of the Pope. *You occupy a place of honor in the Church,* because you have a special part in the mystery of Christ's Cross, the Cross that, in faith, we know is the *tree of eternal life.*

Suffering and illness, and death itself, are part of the mystery of life. But though they may remain a mystery, they should not necessarily remain without meaning. If we join our sufferings to Christ, *they can become an act of love for the Father,* a loving act of giving ourselves up to God's Providence.

I often meet people who tell me that they offer up their prayers and their sacrifices for me and for my wishes. I am profoundly grateful for this gesture of solidarity and devotion, and humbled by the kindness and the generous love of those who suffer. Be assured that the ready acceptance of *your suffering in union with Christ cloaks something extremely valuable to the Church.* If the salvation of the world came from the suffering and death of Jesus, we can be certain how important is the contribution made to the mission of the Church by the sick and by old people, by those who are confined to hospital beds, by invalids in their wheelchairs, by those who share fully in the Cross of the Lord who saves.

CANADA,
SEPTEMBER 15, 1984

93

Sooner or later
sorrow knocks at our door
and, even if we don't want to open to it,
it enters tragically into our existence.
Christian faith
tells us not to lose heart,
but to maintain a deep and living hope,
to trust in God
who neither abandons nor forgets,
to look at Jesus crucified,
the divine Word incarnate
who wanted to suffer like us and for us.
Then the desire,
which cannot be realized,
becomes a hope for quick and complete healing.
All of us know in fact
how precious health is, which enables us to work,
to be interested in various activities,
to pledge ourselves to the needs
of the family and society,
to bring our concrete
and effective contribution
to the development and progress of society.

MARCH 23, 1985

Suffering is the obligatory pathway to salvation and holiness. To become holy, we can fail in this or that charism, this or that particular attitude, but we cannot be exempted from suffering. Suffering is a necessary ingredient of sanctity, and so is love. And in fact the love that Christ teaches us and that he was the first to live, giving us an example, is a *crucified love,* a love that atones and saves through suffering.

Love is more important than suffering: it gives suffering its meaning and makes it acceptable. There can be love without suffering. But suffering without love has no meaning; with love — accepted as Christ accepted it, as the Saints accept it — it acquires an inestimable value.

Dear brothers and sisters! May your souls be filled with that evangelical love which transfigures suffering and alleviates it! May the Lord Jesus grant your hearts peace and strength in bearing your trials. May your souls be safe and sound in spite of the torment of your bodies!

I ardently entreat the Lord that you may be cured; but I also ask for inner grace, which is the life of the soul. I ask that you may be ready to accept the mysterious divine will. I ask that you may struggle to the end.

I ask that you leave enlightened by the evangelical meaning of suffering: here in fact is the central and original value of all Christian morality, and of the true wisdom in life, that Christ taught us and was the first to live. Here is the spring, the decisive force, beyond every virtuous action, of our eternal salvation, and it maintains its meaning and its value forever.

TURIN,
SEPTEMBER 4, 1988

Suffering as Vocation

Suffering is a vocation

As I walk among you, I have noticed a special presence of Christ, of Christ who suffered and who redeemed us with his Cross. You see, this meeting of ours is truly filled with the mystery of redemption, that extraordinary event which took place nineteen hundred and fifty years ago and on which the fate of the world depended and still does. Your suffering places you at the heart of this mystery: it places you, therefore, at the heart of the world, because you are so close to crucified Christ.

As I look at you, dear sick people, my thoughts go out to those who, like you, are at this moment afflicted by suffering. I wish to address myself to them as well, to tell them of my affection and to express the gratitude of the Church, which sees in them a chosen company among the People of God journeying on the paths of history to the blessed domain of Heaven.

Suffering is truly a vocation: it is a call to accept the weight of suffering in order to transform it into a sacrifice of purification and peace offered to the Father in Christ and with Christ, for the salvation of oneself and others.

JUNE 5, 1983

Suffering is a mysterious call

Suffering is a vocation to love more: it is a mysterious call to share in the infinite love of God for mankind, that love which led God to become flesh and to die nailed to the Cross!

The society we live in is tormented by so many problems: the multitude of ideologies, the variety of anthropologies, the complexity of social and political events, the fragmentary nature of personal experiences, the tendency to selfishness, the spread of permissiveness, and, at the same time, anxiety, dissatisfaction, and fear of the future have created a situation so complicated and difficult that we increasingly feel a need to believe the enlightening and saving message of Christ, to love in his name, and to invoke the mercy of the Almighty. The times urge us to accept our cross with courage and serenity, in order to bear witness to the presence of God in human history, revive the meaning of eternity, and instill hope and trust.

"Grant, O my God! that I may adore in silence the order of thy adorable providence in the direction of my life": so said Pascal in the famous Prayer to Ask of God the Proper Use of Sickness. And asking the Lord for his divine consolations, he added: "Grant, my God, that in a constantly equal uniformity of spirit I may receive all kinds of events . . . that such as I am I may conform myself to thy will; and that being sick as I am, I may glorify thee in my sufferings."

Especially today, in modern society, we can see the immense value of Christian suffering, and every local community must carry out the "pastoral of suffering," fully incorporating the sick and suffering into the various apostolic initiatives and activities.

MAY 23, 1987

You are Christ's chosen

The Lord has assigned to you *a singular mission:* to remind each one of us that *suffering has a mysterious value* in the providential design of redemption. What to the eyes of man often appears of little account is before God important and full of merit. You must learn how to see your life with the eyes of God; ask him for the light necessary to comprehend his plans and the strength of mind to embrace his will. May the heavenly Father help you to make of your suffering a gift and service to the Church for the salvation of the world. Repeat often: "Lord, do not be far from me." And: "I place my hope in the Lord."

In Gethsemane and on Calvary Jesus demonstrated the enormity of the outrage of suffering and death, but at the same time he uttered the act of final abandonment into the hands of the Father, and so suffering was joined to love.

UDINE,
MAY 3, 1992

The dignity and majesty of those who suffer

Christ who says to those who suffer "Come and follow me" is the same Christ who suffers: Christ in Gethsemane, Christ scourged, Christ crowned with thorns, Christ on the road of the Cross, Christ on the Cross.

If he says to each one of you, dear brothers and sisters, "Come and follow me," he invites you and calls you to share in the same transformation, the same transmutation of the evil of suffering into the good of salvation: of redemption, of grace, of purification, of conversion . . . for oneself and for others.

For that very reason, St. Paul, who wanted so passionately to imitate Christ, declares elsewhere: "In my flesh I complete what is lacking in Christ's afflictions."

Each of you can make these words the essence of your life and of your vocation.

I wish for you a transformation that is "an inner miracle," even greater than the miracle of healing, a transformation that corresponds to the normal path of God's economy of salvation, as Jesus Christ introduced it to us. I hope and pray that each one of you may find this grace, dear brothers and sisters.

FEBRUARY 11, 1979

The missionary meaning of suffering

If Christ brought about the redemption of mankind through the Cross and suffered in place of man and for man, every man "is called to share in that suffering through which all human suffering was redeemed. In bringing about redemption through suffering, Christ at the same time elevated human suffering to the level of redemption. Hence, too, every man in his suffering can become part of the redemptive suffering of Christ."

I would actively like to urge all the faithful to value suffering in its many forms, joining it to the sacrifice on the Cross for the purpose of evangelization, that is, for the redemption of those who still do not know Christ.

There are millions of brothers and sisters who do not know the Gospel and do not enjoy the immense treasures in the heart of the Redeemer. For them suffering doesn't have a sufficient explanation; it is the most oppressive and inexplicable absurdity and is in tragic contrast with man's aspiration to complete happiness.

Only the Cross of Christ projects a ray of light on this mystery; only in the Cross can humanity find a valid answer to the anguished question that arises from the experience of pain.

I therefore invite all the faithful who suffer — and no one is exempt from pain — to give this apostolic and missionary meaning to their suffering.

MESSAGE FOR WORLD MISSIONARY DAY,
JUNE 10, 1984

Your present suffering is not vain, and certainly it is not absurd. Christ the Lord, who in the Incarnation assumed not only our human nature but also suffering and death, calls all men, and in particular you who are weak and in pain, to work with him for the salvation of the world. Your mysterious *vocation to suffering* is a vocation to love: to love God the Father of mercy, and others, your brothers and sisters. Only the Cross of Christ can illuminate our feeble intelligence and enable it to glimpse the deep meaning of the human and Christian fruitfulness of pain.

The hospital is not only a place of suffering accompanied by hope but also the place where we struggle to make that hope become a reality as soon as possible. The work of healing tends by its nature to defend the life and promote the health of any human being who is in trouble. To that purpose, doctors took the ancient Hippocratic Oath, which in a central passage says: "I will apply dietetic measures for the benefit of the sick according to my ability and judgment; I will keep them from harm and injustice. I will neither give a deadly drug to anybody who asked for it, nor will I make a suggestion to this effect. Similarly I will not give to a woman an abortive remedy."

DECEMBER 20, 1981

Dear sick people, the chosen among believers, *the Church recognizes you as its dearly beloved children!* You are at the center of Christ's work for salvation because in a concrete way you share the Cross of every day and carry it behind him. Your contribution is crucial for the coming of the Kingdom of God. Trustfully abandoning yourselves to heavenly Providence, you constantly remind us of the essential word of the evangelical message, proposing to all the narrow road of faith that leads to the ultimate goal; you demonstrate that there is no truer declaration, no greater gift, no more intense desire than to seek an answer there where it seems impossible.

In the paschal mystery, *the mystery of the Cross and of glory, victory passes through an apparent defeat,* life vanquishes death, love triumphs over every violence, forgiveness destroys sin. The Cross is the source of serenity and of peace, of comfort and of apostolic boldness: may it be so especially for you, dearest sick people.

CREMA,
JUNE 20, 1992

We can actively contribute to the expansion of the Kingdom of Christ and the development of his mystical body in a threefold direction:

—by learning to give to our own suffering a genuine purpose, rooted in the dynamism of the Church's participation in the redeeming work of Christ;

—by inviting our brothers and sisters who suffer in body and soul to understand this apostolic dimension of suffering and, as a result, to invest their trials, and their pain, with a sense of mission;

—by making our own, with inexhaustible charity, the pain that daily afflicts such a large proportion of humanity, those who are tormented by illness, by hunger, by persecution, who are deprived of fundamental and inalienable rights, such as liberty; that is, suffering mankind, in whom we must distinguish the face of Christ, the "Man of sorrows," and whom we must try to comfort as well as we can.

JUNE 10, 1984

The Good Samaritan

I would now like to express my feelings of appreciation to those who do their utmost for you, dearest sick people, surrounding you with their loving attention: the doctors, the nurses, and all those who perform the services that are necessary during pilgrimages and in your homes or hospitals, and also, above all, your families, on whom the greatest burden falls.

Like the servants at Cana, who "knew"—as the steward of the feast did not—of the miracle performed by Jesus, may those who help you be always aware of the miracle of grace that is fulfilled in your lives and may they help you to be equal to the task that God has entrusted to you.

FEBRUARY 11, 1980

The "word of the Cross" has a message for you health-care workers, who, at various levels and with varying responsibilities, do your jobs in hospitals.

It is Jesus Christ who hides and is revealed in the face and in the flesh, in the heart and in the soul of those whom you are called to help and to care for. He considers done to himself what is done to the least of these brothers, who are ill and often alone and marginalized by society.

This requires of you words, gestures, and inner attitudes inspired not only by a profound and rich humanity but by a genuine spirit of faith and charity.

I therefore ask you and, through you, all those who work in health-care facilities, to overcome the temptation to indifference and selfishness and to do your utmost above all *to humanize these health-care environments and make them more livable,* in such a way that the sick may be cured in the totality of their body and soul. Do your utmost so that all the *fundamental rights and values of the human being* may be recognized and supported, and above all the right to life, from its beginning to its natural end. That requires attention to different situations, respectful and patient dialogue, generous love for every man and woman considered as the image of God and, for those who are believers, an "icon" of Christ who suffers.

APRIL 1, 1990

I wish to express to the doctors, nurses, and health-care aides my deep appreciation and respect for the skill and attention they bring to the practice of their professions. This is a true vocation, undertaken for the care of our brothers and sisters who suffer. Few other professions are so worthy and honorable as that of the doctor who works with commitment and has strong ethical and humanitarian feelings. It approaches a sort of priesthood whose mission consists in healing the body and also in comforting the soul.

Thus I urge these professionals to be aware of the value of their mission, always to serve life and never death, to be completely honest in the choice of treatments and surgical interventions, not to yield to the temptation for money, not to abandon their country for purely material gains, and to see in their patients — even the poorest, who at times cannot pay for their services — human beings and children of God.

I commend to the Lord all those who work on behalf of the sick in hospitals, clinics, and hospices. I wish to repeat to all, doctors, nurses, chaplains, and hospital personnel: yours is a noble vocation. Remember that you serve Christ in the sufferings of your brothers and sisters.

BOLIVIA,
MAY 12, 1988

May the sick person be your university

The sick, the suffering, and the needy, who are sometimes a cause of irritation, or even an obstacle, become for those who have faith the people we love most, because they are living signs of the presence of God. Making room for the other, practicing the charism of hospitality will mean, in a certain sense, making room for Christ and enabling him to live with you and in you.

Those who suffer and toward whom you practice your "compassion" have much to teach you to transform your existence as Religious: let the sick person be your university!

To the Chapter of the Order of the Fatebenefratelli, November 25, 1988

You, both male and female religious, have dedicated yourselves to bringing hope and healing, in the name of Christ, to the sick and the poor, to the old and the illiterate — to every member of society who is suffering — without distinction of race, belief, or social position. Through you the Church pursues Christ's work of healing. I pray that many young men and women may join your ranks and maintain unchanged through the generations to come the charism of service to the sick. You have a special place in the heart of Jesus and the heart of the Church.

AUSTRALIA,
NOVEMBER 28, 1986

The priest is called to visit the sick

The priest is called to follow the example of Christ and to bring to the sick all the sympathy of the Savior.

Unlike Christ, he does not have the power to heal the sick and the infirm, but he can obtain for them moral and spiritual comfort, which will sustain them in their trials, and also facilitate the pace of healing. With prayer, the priest will ask for and obtain improvement in the health of the sick who are entrusted to him.

His pastoral ministry leads him to bring love to the most wretched, as the Gospel particularly urges him to do. Every time the priest visits a sick person, he is asked to discover in him the mysterious presence of Christ: "I was sick and you visited me."

In the sufferings of the sick person he will acknowledge, with love and respect, the mystery of Christ crucified, which is extended into human lives.

The priest is called to visit the sick in this perspective of the work of salvation. Jesus performed many miraculous cures as signs of the cures that he wished to obtain for mankind. He did not make the healing of the body an absolute purpose: he wished to save men from evil. Thus we see that he forgives the sins of the paralytic before curing him, and performs the miracle in order to demonstrate the reality of that forgiveness. The priest must always have in view the goal of his mission, the total salvation of the man, which has, first of all, a spiritual dimension. He must be aware that illness is a time of trial but also of grace, and he must encourage the sick to take advantage of this grace to draw closer to Christ, to discover his mysterious presence, to accept the will of the Father, and to offer him their sufferings more generously.

Let us pray to the Virgin Mary, whose heart is so compassionate, that she may maternally guide the priests in their visits, and inspire them unceasingly in this important ministry.

AUGUST 12, 1990

"Do simple things in a grand way"

We must not fall into the error of evaluating our lives solely on the basis of tangible results. No life is without value. The simple things of life, daily work in cooperation with others, the kindness of those who help their neighbors and appreciation on the part of those who are helped — these are facts that possess great importance in the light of the life of Jesus, transforming us into witnesses of the Good News.

That is the extraordinary thing which saturates the hidden divine force, the force that enables us to flourish wherever we are sown. We are called on to be great in small things. It is also the attitude of Mary, who at the angel's announcement said: "Behold I am the handmaid of the Lord, let it be to me according to your word."

We must look for gold in the earth that is under our feet, which means to value the life that the Lord has allotted us.

HOLLAND,
MAY 13, 1985

Make medicine more humane

Since it is part of the tradition of the Church to consider Christian everything that is authentically human, I feel it is my duty to call on you urgently to make your practice of medicine more humane, and to establish a frank bond of solidarity with your patients, one that goes beyond a professional relationship. The sick person secretly expects this from you. Besides, he stands before you in all his nobility as a human being who, in spite of being needy, suffering, and perhaps even crippled, should not for that reason be considered a passive object. On the contrary, a person is always a subject and should be approached as such. This is the inborn dignity of man. A person by his nature needs a personal relationship. Even someone who is sick is never just a clinical case but always a "sick *person*"; he expects competent and effective care from you, but he also expects the capacity and skill to inspire trust, even to the point where you can discuss the situation honestly with him and, above all, display a sincere attitude of "sym-pathy" (feeling with), in the etymological sense of the word, so as to translate into practice the words of the Apostle Paul, which echoed those of an ancient wise man: "Rejoice with those who are happy, weep with those who are in pain."

AT A MEDICAL CONVENTION ON
THE TREATMENT OF TUMORS,
FEBRUARY 25, 1982

I wish to greet you and thank you, too, dear directors and members of the National Unitalsi Association and of Opera Romana Pellegrinaggi,* whose assiduous, discreet, disinterested, and generous work I know and value. Not only today but every day you undertake a task that, beyond any limiting sociological or professional qualification, has a clearly defined and honored name in the Christian vocabulary: charity, as an exercise of evangelical care for our weaker brothers, care that is given to them in the name of God and his son Jesus. *Infirmis (eram) et visitastis me* . . . I thank you also in the name of those who, at times, have neither voice nor strength to thank you themselves.

FEBRUARY 11, 1982

---

*These are two organizations that help sick people make pilgrimages to such places as Lourdes.

I love you with all the strength and tenderness of my affection, even if it's impossible for me to lend you a hand! I see in you persons who suffer, who have an anxious, ineradicable longing for health and physical well-being, and who justly cling to the work of doctors and the results of science; I love you, because in you is the mysterious but true presence of Christ. One cannot help being sensitive in the face of suffering!

Therefore welcome this fraternal greeting, which I offer warmly, and you may be certain that among the various encounters scheduled for this pastoral visit, all of which I look forward to, the personal contact with you, the sick, is assuredly among the most important.

It is a cause of joy to know that many volunteers offer their help to the sick. Unitalsi, Oftal, the Volunteers of Suffering, the Diocesan Association for Aid to the Sick have been active for a long time in the dioceses. Other men and women who are not members of organizations, also devote their time to the sick.

Let me praise these beneficial initiatives, which transform Christian faith into living charity, and I encourage you all to be always and in every instance like the good Samaritan of the Gospel, because the world today has an urgent need for this testimony of love.

ORISTANO,
OCTOBER 18, 1985

Make medicine and hospitals more humane

In every part of the world we see vigorous growth in the phenomenon of the volunteer, with a great number of persons, especially among the young, offering to spend at least part of their time working, without pay, on behalf of the community. For Christians, to take on that responsibility for the common good is a practical way of demonstrating their willingness to follow the example of Christ by sharing the problems and difficulties of their brothers and sisters.

How can we fail to give proper thanks to the important contribution that the loving and modest presence of volunteers brings to the promise of healing and care, complementing the work of the nursing personnel?

Volunteer service, if properly coordinated, can help to improve the quality of care, adding an extra touch of human warmth and attention, which can obviously comfort the patient and perhaps even have a positive effect on the outcome of the treatment.

I know that in a considerable number of Catholic hospitals, especially in the wards for the chronically ill, much has been done in this field.

But the present circumstances would seem to suggest that it is time to make an attempt to broaden the use of the generous resources available in the community, and to this purpose it would be useful for hospitals run on a Christian basis to share their aspirations. The goal is a structure of health-care assistance that is not isolated but, rather, a vital part of the social fabric that surrounds it. An active exchange between the community of the healthy and the community of the sick will surely provide a powerful incentive for an increase in charity.

The Catholic hospitals are charged with great responsibilities at the moment, and their survival depends on the fact that Catholics occupy themselves not only with the sick but with all people. Their survival, similarly, depends on this: on whether Catholics can create a new culture and new forms of pastoral assistance for the sick, testifying to the fact that Christ is the savior of the soul as well as of the body.

TO THE HEALTH-CARE WORKERS
IN CATHOLIC HOSPITALS,
OCTOBER 31, 1985

You, dear relatives and friends of the sick, you are like those who led the sick to Jesus.

You bear along with them their illness, their infirmity, their physical disability, and even more, perhaps, in the case of an irreversible mental disability.

I entreat the Lord to help you in this generous and delicate assistance, which engages all the resources of your love. This assistance can extend to sharing the prayers of the sick person and seeking out others who can give him the necessary spiritual support — priest, deacon, nun, lay friend, or one who is charged with pastoral service to sick people.

This service to the sick is in fact one of the priorities that are imposed on your Christian communities. Numerous institutions make marvelous contributions in this field. Groups of people who visit the sick have here a fundamental task. But they must be present in the life of the parishes more generally. Let us do as much as possible so that, in their way and according to their capabilities, those who are sick can take part in the prayers of the community and its initiatives. Let us not ignore the human and spiritual energy that the sick are often endowed with. With them, we contribute to the grace of suffering.

BELGIUM,
MAY 21, 1985

The Prayer of the Sick

The Cross is the instrument of redemption

The Church places great trust in the contribution of your prayers and your sufferings. They constitute a precious treasure that is drawn on by the entire community of believers, which is in need of light and support. Always have a lively consciousness of the important role that you are called on to play in the mystical body of Christ.

If the sufferings brought on by illness are your cross, do not refuse to embrace it with strength of spirit, as Jesus did during the journey on the Via Crucis and on Calvary: for you and for the world the Cross is the instrument of Redemption and salvation. Offer your suffering for the benefit of the Church.

Dear brothers and sisters, I hope that you will regain your health, so that you may return home and take up your occupations. Your loved ones await you, and you can still do so much for them.

Yet, as long as illness keeps you in the hospital, learn how to make this time spiritually valuable. I wish to leave you today with an assignment: collaborate with Christ and the Church, collaborate with the Pope in his ministry in the service of the people of God. Be near me with the offering of your sacrifices, in which the saving power of Christ's Cross is active. For your solidarity, for your support, I am profoundly grateful.

MESTRE,
JUNE 17, 1985

I ask for your prayers, which are especially pleasing to God.

Pray for all those in the world who suffer.

Pray for peace. Pray for the Church, as it prays for you. Remember all those who have preceded you in faith; Mary our Mother, who watches over us, and the Saints, whose lives reveal the power of God which shines through human weakness. Remember them and have no fear.

AUSTRALIA,
NOVEMBER 25, 1989

All of you have a *special apostolate,* to be united with God and pray for those who do not know him. I ask you to pray for me and for the Catholic Church throughout the world. I ask you to pray for those who cannot pray and do not know how to, and for all those who have lost faith in God and his mercy.

Let the light and the presence of Christ who heals shine in your lives so that all who come in contact with you may discover the sweetness of God who loves us.

FINLAND,
JUNE 6, 1989

Yet again I ask you from my heart, dear sick Christian brothers, who are old and suffering, *to sustain, in proportion to your strength, and with devout fortitude in your sufferings, the work of the Church with your prayers, and with your sacrifices,* here and throughout the world. The Pope himself, in his particular pastoral activity, relies heavily on your active contribution. And pray above all that the Lord may send enough workers into his vineyard, so that his name may be worthily praised everywhere.

LIECHTENSTEIN,
SEPTEMBER 8, 1985

Raise to the Almighty, through the intercession of our heavenly Mother, your prayers and your sufferings for the salvation of souls! Modern man has an urgent need for firm and confident faith. The phenomenon of "secularization" does not, in the end, fulfill, does not satisfy, and leaves modern man disappointed and anxious for genuine, assured truth. With your life and your prayers, may you be the precious oil, thanks to which, in the Church and in every Christian, the lamp of faith and charity shines forever!

Dearest ones! After the apparitions of Our Lady, little Bernadette Soubirous* lived with a piercing nostalgia for Heaven. She often repeated: "Let's go to Heaven, let's work for Heaven, all the rest is nothing!"

And she added, "Heaven, I must earn it!"

I, too, wish to exhort you all to look up to Heaven, where our true homeland is, and where a place is prepared for us. May Most Holy Mary illuminate your path, sustain you, and be a comfort to you now and every day of your life. Amen.

FEBRUARY 11, 1983

---

*St. Bernadette, Bernadette Soubirous (1844–79), saw a vision of the Virgin Mary in a cave near Lourdes in 1858. At the site, Bernadette discovered a spring with healing powers. A chapel was built at the cave, the Grotto of Massabielle, and millions of pilgrims visit Lourdes each year. Bernadette Soubirous was canonized by Pope Pius XI in 1933. Her body has lain in a shrine at the Chapel of the Convent of St. Gildard at Nevers since 1925.

I commend to you the Church and the world

As I walked down the nave of the Church, I shook hands with all those who were nearby. Then, through them, this gesture was transmitted to the others. This is a significant sign: I gave you my hands to demonstrate to you that we are joined, or, rather, to show you my deep desire to be more closely joined. I strongly wish for this union with the suffering; it is my strength, because my strength is the Cross of Christ, and the Cross of Christ is present in your suffering.

I wish to embrace all of you, and each one of you, and I would like to be close to each of you. I commend myself to your prayers and your sacrifices. I commend myself, and I commend the whole Church and the world, a world that runs a greater and greater risk, and has always a greater need for the Cross and for redemption. This is why I commend to you the Church and the world, and also my person, the person of the Pope who must serve the Church and the world.

RIMINI,
AUGUST 29, 1982

I invite you to pray for me!

May you especially, you who have been tested by illness, bring the offering of your sufferings and so follow me closely during this journey. You can do so much for me; yet again you can communicate to me that strength I spoke of the day after my election to the See of Rome, and whose inner power I felt, too, during my illness.

I am confident that the help of your prayers will not fail me this time, either, nor will the merit of your sufferings, and for all this I wish to thank you from this moment on. During the Holy Sacrifice, in the communion of charity which is like the breath of life of the Church, I, in turn, will not fail to pray for you and for your health.

FEBRUARY 11, 1982

I ask you to pray and to offer your sufferings for mankind, for the Church, and also for me, so that my universal pastoral service may be fulfilled according to the will of God.

And in the name of mankind, in the name of the Church, and in my name I say to you: "Thanks!" May the Lord, who is rich in mercy, give all of you peace and inner joy and reward with his grace those who with generous disinterest take loving care of you: your families, friends, doctors, nurses, priests, nuns.

TERNI,
MARCH 19, 1981

Pray to be cured

I would like to leave you as a special memory — dear sick people and dear friends who help you — the exhortation of Jesus, the Divine Teacher, on the need to pray always and not lose heart.

It is natural, indeed necessary, to pray first of all to be cured, because health is a great gift of God, a marvelous good, which must be respected and cared for; and many episodes from the Gospel show us how Jesus bent over the sick and cured them. Therefore, pray to be cured; pray for the recovery or at least the relief of the sick.

Yet there are illnesses that have no cure; there are sufferings that drag on through the years and sometimes oppress an entire life with their hopelessness, sufferings in the face of which biology, medicine, and surgery, in spite of their wonderful discoveries and treatments, remain impotent and are defeated. It is at these moments and in these situations that we must pray with a more intense fervor, to preserve our intimacy with God, who appears so mysterious and silent, to call on the strength of resignation, the courage of trusting perseverance, patience in the torment of solitude. Thus prayer becomes a support, a consolation, a comfort. However weak, suffering, and neglected a human creature is, prayer keeps alive and real the bond with the Almighty, who loves like a Father every person created "in his own likeness, after his image," and continues to extend to all his goodness and mercy. "Pray at all times," St. Paul urges. "Let your requests be made known to God."

Pray, then, also for the many needs, both spiritual and temporal, of your families, of your communities, of the whole Church and of all mankind: in fact, prayer is the first and greatest charity that we must perform for our brothers. Especially today, on the eve of the World Day of Prayer for Peace, I urge you to pray fervently for the supreme ideals of Truth and salvation and for peace in the world.

I urge you to pray to Most Holy Mary with filial devotion: holding the crown of the Rosary in your hands, call on Mary, always, and especially in the most painful moments of illness and sorrow.

PERUGIA,
OCTOBER 26, 1986

I call on you to entrust your anguish to God the Father and to Christ, through Mary; to ask of him—more than resignation, and even more than courage for your struggle—*the grace of love and hope*. Look at the Cross of Christ with faith: although it is the instrument of immense suffering, it is above all the sign of immense love, and the open door to Resurrection, which is the ultimate response of the God of love to his chosen Son.

May you *offer* this handicap of yours together with Christ, and enter into redemption: for your salvation, for the progress of the whole Church, for the graces of conversion that our world needs! Remain faithful to *prayer*. Try to remain *open to others*, without turning in on yourselves. Others have a lot to gain from your experience as sick people and as believers. Often, your ordeal has enabled you to acquire an outlook on existence and what is truly valuable, and gain a new degree of patience, of courage, of solidarity, of serenity at the prospect of death—in contrast with the anxiety of those around you—and a mysterious union with God. To all this you can bear witness, making manifest the promise of Jesus: "Blessed are those who mourn, for they shall be comforted." Even in the silence of prayer, and confined to bed, you are in communion with the whole world, in order to take part in redemption: your prayer and your offering help to elevate the world.

BELGIUM,
MAY 21, 1985

Nothing in your suffering is wasted

Following the desire of our Heavenly Mother, we express our love and our trust in her through the Rosary. And so I urge you all to continue the daily recitation of this marvelous prayer, which is truly helpful in our spiritual life. In fact the Rosary, with its meditation on the mysteries, and with its trustful invocation of maternal protection in life and death, comforts us in the commitment to model our Christian life on that of Jesus and Mary; calls on us to imitate them with the help of God's grace; and spurs us to practice all the virtues, especially that of brotherly charity.

The Rosary has immense benefits for every person's spiritual life, for the family environment, and for the social and ecclesial environment of every parish.

Dear faithful, especially those who are sick!

May the Rosary be with you every day so that you may conform to the wishes of Our Lady, as the Saints did!

Together with your friends and relatives, who care for you with loving devotion, I ask for you from the Most Holy Virgin the great gift of health, and the strength to resign yourselves to the will of God.

May Jesus, who says, *"Come unto me, all you who are heavy laden and oppressed, and I will give you rest,"* be a source of comfort and support: abandon yourselves to him with total trust, certain that he will miss none of your pain. If your faith in Christ and in the reality of his presence in those who suffer is deeply rooted, your courage will never fail! We will understand in Heaven the value of human suffering in the plan of Providence for bringing to fulfillment the "story of salvation."

Finally, I wish to entrust to your prayer and your intentions all the needs of the Church. Your apostolate of prayer and suffering is surely indispensable for the good of the Church: you, too, are in the front lines of support in the work of evangelization, conversion, and sanctification in the world.

Dear sick ones! I entrust to you the job of praying for the Church, for the Pope, for priestly and religious vocations.

SEPTEMBER 6, 1986

Sick people and the Rosary

I heartily urge you, sick people and all the rest of you, friends, relatives, priests, and religious, to pray to Our Lady every day with the Holy Rosary.

Since health is a good that is part of the original plan of creation, to recite the Rosary for sick people, so that they may be cured or at least obtain relief from their suffering, is an exquisitely Christian and human service; it is always consoling and always effective, because it instills serenity and strength of spirit. And when the illness persists and suffering remains, the Rosary also reminds us that the redemption of mankind is brought about by means of the Cross. Meditation on the mysteries of salvation, which has been obtained for us on the Cross of the Redeemer, who became flesh for love of us, gives us a fundamental understanding of the value of suffering for the Church, for the return to grace of those who live in error and sin, and for the conversion of those who are alienated from God, from Christ, or from the Church. The silent, hidden suffering of a sick person is worth more than all the clamor of many discussions and arguments. "A spark of pure love," St. John of the Cross wrote, "is more precious in the eyes of God and in those of the soul than any other thing; love is the purpose for which we were created. Without prayer and without union with God, everything is reduced to a pointless hammering, and we seem to be doing little more than nothing, and sometimes in fact nothing, indeed, often we may even be doing harm." We read, in the biography of St. Bernadette, that when she recited the Rosary she emphasized in particular the words "Pray for us sinners." To anyone who noticed this, she responded: "Oh, yes! We must pray for sinners. The Holy Virgin urges it. We can never do enough for the conversion of sinners." Since she was almost always ill, Bernadette said: "My task is to be sick: to suffer is my duty. Prayer is my only weapon: I cannot do other than pray and suffer!" And this is also the message left by Our Lady at Fatima for the three children: suffering and the Rosary for the Church and for sinners.

The people who care for the sick may draw from the Rosary the strength to be always kind, loving, and patient toward those who suffer, and respectful of their pain.

ORISTANO,
OCTOBER 18, 1985

With profound faith, the great Blaise Pascal expressed himself thus in the Prayer to Ask of God the Proper Use of Sickness: "Grant, O my God! that I may adore in silence the order of thy adorable providence in the direction of my life.... Grant me the favor, Lord, to join thy consolations to my sufferings, that I may suffer like a Christian.... Neither do I ask to be in the fullness of evils without consolation; for this is the state of Judaism. But I ask, Lord, to feel at the same time both the sorrows of nature for my sins, and the consolations of thy spirit through thy grace."

And St. Bernadette Soubirous, who in her girlhood often went hungry, and who knew how precious bread is, prayed thus: "O Jesus, give me, I pray you, the bread of humility, the bread of obedience, the bread of charity!... O Jesus, you wish to crucify me: Let it be! Give me the bread of the strength to suffer, the bread of seeing only you in everything and forever. Jesus, Mary, the Cross: I want no other friends but these!"

Truly, the Gospel, as a message of absolute and ultimate truth, is also the message of genuine joy, because it gives meaning and value to our sufferings.

FEBRUARY 11, 1983

For my part, I rely on you: as I ask for the help of the prayers of the monks and the nuns and many other holy persons that the Spirit may inspire and give strength to my pontifical ministry, so I ask the precious help that can come to me from the offering of your sufferings and your illness. May this offering be joined to your prayers; or, rather, transformed into prayers for me, for my immediate coworkers, and for all those who entrust to me their afflictions and their sorrows, their needs and their wants.

But why not begin this prayer immediately?
Lord,
with the faith that you have given us,
we confess to you, omnipotent God,
our Creator and provident Father,
God of hope
in Jesus Christ our Savior,
God of love,
in the Holy Spirit, our Consoler!

Lord,
trusting in your promises
that are eternal,
we wish to come to you always,
to find in you
relief from our suffering.

Yet,
being disciples of Jesus,
we cannot do as we wish,

but do your will
in all our living!

Lord,
grateful for the love
of Christ
for the lepers who have had
the good fortune to come in contact with Him,
we see ourselves in them . . .
we thank you also for the encouragement
we receive in everything that helps us,
brings us relief, and comforts us:
we thank you
for the medicine and the doctors,
for the care and the nurses,
for our living conditions,
for those who comfort us
and who are by us comforted,
for those who understand us
and accept us for the others.

Lord,
grant us patience, serenity, and courage;
allow us to live a joyful charity,
for your love,
toward those who suffer more than we do
and toward those who, not suffering,
do not have a clear sense of the meaning of life.

Lord,
we want our life to be useful,
we wish to serve:
to praise, thank,
shelter, and pray, with Christ,
for those who adore you
and for those who do not adore you,
in the world, and for your Church,
scattered throughout the earth.

Lord,
through the infinite merits of Christ
on the Cross, your "suffering servant"
and our brother, with whom we are joined,
we pray to you for our families,
friends, and benefactors,
and for good results from the Pope's visit
and for Brazil. So let it be.

BRAZIL,
JULY 8, 1980

Offering of the self

O Lord,
may my soul
be flooded with your light
so that I may know you more profoundly!
Lord,
give me so much love,
love forever, serene and generous,
love that will join me to you always!
Lord,
grant that I may serve you,
serve you truly and well,
on the paths that you wish to open up
to my existence down here.

Christ of our sufferings,
Christ of our sacrifices,
Christ of our Gethsemane,
Christ of our difficult transformations,
Christ of our faithful service to our neighbor,
Christ of our pilgrimages to Lourdes,
Christ of our community,
Christ our Redeemer,
Christ our brother!
Amen.

For the sick

Lord of life,
take the sick by the hand
and help them in their trials,
comfort them in hardship and in pain,
bestow on them your joy as a reward
for the sufferings embraced by them
for love of their brothers,
in total adherence to your redeeming Cross.
Grant that their prayers
and acceptance of their suffering
may be a source of new vocations for the Church.

Let us therefore pray that the Holy Spirit may grant you the *strength of faith* to believe always in the Lord who saves us: the *strength of hope* to trust fully in his aid and in his kindness toward us; the *strength of love* to love the Lord more and more, and with all our hearts and to love, in him and for him, your brothers and sisters; the *strength of patience* to be able to accept your condition with courage and by offering your sufferings for the good of our souls; the *strength of the good example,* so that to others you may bear witness of charity and hope.

APRIL 11, 1981

I pray every day in a special way for all of you who are called "to complete" with your sufferings "what is lacking in Christ's afflictions."

I would like to add that I do it every day at the most emotional moment of the Holy Mass, when the time for Communion approaches. I think that just at that point all sick people should be particularly close to Jesus and Jesus should be particularly close to all who are sick and suffering, so that they may be embraced in a special way by this Communion, our salvation, which is the Eucharist.

POLAND,
JUNE 6, 1991

Mary—
Health of the Sick

My beloved brothers and sisters, Mary is always with you, just as she was at the foot of the Cross of Jesus.

Turn to her, and tell her your troubles. The hand and the maternal gaze of the Virgin will give you relief and comfort you, as only she knows how to do.

When you recite the Holy Rosary, place special emphasis on the invocation of the litany "Health of the Sick, pray for us."

In the Holy Mass that I will celebrate today, I will commend everyone to the Lord and especially you, dear sick people; your sufferings will be on the altar, an offering to Christ at the same time.

ARGENTINA,
APRIL 8, 1987

Look at your destiny with the eyes of faith

Mary is at your side because she herself suffered with her divine Son. The face of the mother of sorrows is familiar to all of us, and we carry it stamped deeply in our hearts: the dead body of the divine Son lies in the lap of his grieving Mother, that womb from which he came into the light. The maternal heart of Mary is pierced with grief; because no one is as close to a son as his mother. But the heavenly Father, who does not abandon men even in their hardest trials, gave the Mother of Jesus the strength to persevere at the Cross and to take part in the Passion of her son.

The worship of Our Lady of Sorrows can be a source of strength for you, so that you may accept life's burdens with devotion, and through prayer and meditation join them consciously to the Passion and death of the Lord. If you bear your daily struggles and hardships patiently, you sanctify not only yourselves but, at the same time, the Church and the world. *Suffering accepted for the love of Christ is always suffering for salvation.* Yes, as the faithful of Christ, we, too, must try to understand and live the meaning and dignity of human suffering.

LIECHTENSTEIN,
SEPTEMBER 8, 1985

You, too, dearest sick people, place yourselves under the Blessed Virgin's protective mantle, and you, too, ask her for comfort. And you are right to do so. Aren't the horsemen of the Apocalypse forever on the road, under forever new names? Even if we have never experienced pestilence, or plague, there are many other illnesses and ordeals that afflict men today. Despite all the progress of medicine, incurable diseases still exist, and often cause overwhelming anguish. And doesn't the scourge of war, which has struck us so many times, loom over the world today, with the threat of millions dead and unimaginable destruction? And who is not familiar with the terrifying images of hunger that we see every day in so many regions of the earth? In all these situations of hardship and suffering, and in so many others that I cannot enumerate here, we as believers must seek refuge in Mary, just as our fathers before us did. Yes, my dear ones, let us pray always and at all times: Holy Mary Mother of God, pray for us. That does not mean averting our gaze from problems, nor is it a matter of fleeing in the face of need or danger; it is simply Christian trust in the help of God, who gave us Mary as our mother. And does a mother exist whose children cannot ask her for help?

LUXEMBOURG,
MAY 15, 1985

With your suffering you purify the Church

Christianity is woven of suffering and joy, of passion and resurrection.

Dear sick people, know how to welcome this spiritual message. The most Holy Virgin, whom we venerate in the mystery of her appearances at Lourdes, is a magnificent example for us. She is at the foot of the Cross, joined in a remarkable way to the sacrifice of her Son: she is the mother of sorrows. But she is also open to the joy of resurrection; she is assumed, body and soul, into the glory of Heaven. Immaculate from her conception, she is the first creature to be redeemed, and is the perfect model of the earthly Church and the glorified Church.

She therefore exhorts us to courage and trust, and reminds us that we cannot find joy without traveling along the obligatory path of suffering: *"Per crucem ad lucem"*: "By means of the Cross to the light." Your life is not different from that of Our Lady and that of St. Bernadette; look at it with their eyes. Illness is not a useless fate; it is not something that oppresses us without leaving any trace of something positive.

On the contrary, if it is borne in communion with Christ, it becomes a source of hope, of salvation, and of resurrection for you and for all mankind.

FEBRUARY II, 1985

154

Mary leads you to the encounter with Christ

Know that Most Holy Mary, Mother of the Redeemer and our mother, wants to lead you to Christ the Liberator. Guided, day after day, by her maternal hand, you are called to a constantly renewed encounter with Christ, who delivers us from evil.

As the Letter to the Hebrews says: "Therefore, strengthen your feeble arms and weak knees. Make level paths for your feet, so that the lame may not be disabled, but rather healed."

Dearest sick people, ask Most Holy Mary the liberator for the grace to understand, and to help those near you to understand, that deliverance is ephemeral and illusory if it does not free us from the root of evil and death, which is sin.

While you pray for the health of body and soul, offer your sufferings to Christ of the Passover, through Most Holy Mary, so that you, too, may become, together with him, instruments of deliverance from every form of evil that oppresses man and the world.

May the Most Holy Virgin be your light and hope forever, and direct your thoughts toward that homeland where neither evil nor death exists.

VITERBO,
MAY 27, 1984

We look at Mary just as Elizabeth did, seeing her arrive with a hurried step and hearing her voice in greeting: "As soon as the sound of your greeting reached my ears, the baby in my womb leaped for joy."

How can we not meditate on this first call to reflection? Elizabeth's leap for joy points out the gift that can be contained in a simple greeting, when it comes from a heart overflowing with God. How often can the darkness of solitude, which oppresses a soul, be pierced by the luminous ray of a smile and a kind word!

A kind word is quickly said; and yet at times it is difficult for us to utter it. Weariness deters us, anxiety constricts us, a feeling of coldness or of selfish indifference restrains us. Thus it happens that we pass by even people we know without looking them in the face and without realizing how often they are suffering from that subtle, debilitating pain that comes from feeling ignored. A cordial word would be enough, an affectionate gesture, and immediately something would reawaken in them: a nod of attention and politeness can be a gust of fresh air in the mustiness of an existence that is oppressed by sadness and discouragement. Mary's greeting filled her old cousin Elizabeth's heart with joy.

FEBRUARY 11, 1981

Know that you are not alone, or cut off, or abandoned on your Via Crucis; beside you, beside each one of you, is the Immaculate Virgin, who considers you her most beloved children: Mary, who "became for us Mother in the order of grace . . . from the consent which she loyally gave at the Annunciation and which she sustained without wavering beneath the Cross," is near you, because she suffered deeply with Jesus for the salvation of the world.

Look at her with full trust and filial abandon; she looks at you with a special gaze, she smiles at you with maternal tenderness, and lovingly cares for you!

May this sweet Mother help you and protect you: we pray to her for you, that she may be near you, comfort you, give you peace and lead to the fulfillment in you — for the good of the Church, for the spread of the Gospel, for peace in the world — of that design of grace and love, which more tightly binds and configures you to Jesus Christ. I'm sure that you will pray for the Pope and will also offer your sufferings to the Lord, right? In that way, our friendly conversation will continue beyond this brief space of time.

MAY 21, 1979

The message of Lourdes

At Lourdes, Mary reminded the world that the meaning of life on earth is its orientation toward Heaven.

Our Lady, at Lourdes, came to speak to man of "paradise," so that although he was actively engaged in the building of a more welcoming and a more just world, he would not forget to lift his eyes to Heaven to draw from it guidance and hope.

The Most Holy Virgin came, furthermore, to remind us of the value of conversion and penance, again presenting to the world the heart of the evangelical message. She said to Bernadette, during the appearance of February 18: "I promise to make you happy not in this world but in the next." Later, she asked her to pray for the conversion of sinners and on February 24 she repeated three times: "Penance, penance, penance!"

At Lourdes, Mary emphatically points out the reality of the redemption of mankind from sin through the Cross, which is to say through suffering. God himself, having become man, wished to die innocent, nailed to a cross!

At Lourdes, Our Lady teaches the redemptive value of suffering; it bestows courage, patience, resignation; it illuminates the mystery of our participation in the passion of Christ; it raises our inner gaze to true and complete happiness, which Jesus himself has assured and prepared for us beyond life and history. Bernadette had understood Mary's message perfectly, and had become a nun in Nevers. She was gravely ill, but when anyone entreated her to go to the grotto of Massabielle to pray for a cure she answered: "Lourdes is not for me!" She was subject to powerful asthmatic attacks, and when a novice nurse asked her, "Do you suffer a lot?" she answered simply: "It is necessary!" Ultimately, the message of Lourdes is completed by the invitation to prayer: Mary appears in the attitude of praying, asks Bernadette to recite the Rosary with her own personal crown, asks her to build a chapel there, and to have people come in procession.

This, too, is an admonition that is still valid. Our Lady of Lourdes came to tell us, with the authority and kindness of a Mother, that if we truly want to sustain, strengthen, and spread the Christian faith, humble, trustful prayer is needed.

FEBRUARY 11, 1987

Faith alleviates suffering

At Lourdes Mary undertakes as her mission the relief of suffering and the reconciliation of our souls with God and our neighbor.

The graces that this Mother of mercy obtains for the immense crowds of suffering, lost humanity all have the purpose of leading men and women to Christ and obtaining for them the gift of his Spirit.

At Lourdes Mary, through St. Bernadette, revealed herself conspicuously as "the voice of the will of the Son."

Everything that Our Lady said to the Seer, everything that she urged her to do, everything that began at Lourdes, that happened and is happening there, reflects, if you wish, the "will" of Our Lady: but in whose name has She obtained all this, in whose grace, if not that of her divine Son?

So we can say that Lourdes belongs to Christ even more than to his Most Holy Mother.

At Lourdes we learn to know Christ through Mary. The miracles of Lourdes and the miracles of Christ, achieved through the intercession of Mary.

For this reason Lourdes is an honored place of Christian *experience*.

At Lourdes we learn to suffer as Christ suffered. We accept suffering as he accepted it.

At Lourdes our suffering is alleviated because it is lived with Christ. *Provided* one lives it with Christ, supported by Mary.

At Lourdes we learn that faith does not alleviate suffering in the sense of lessening it physically. This is the task of medicine, or, very rarely, it may happen miraculously.

At Lourdes we learn that faith alleviates suffering by making it acceptable as a means of expiation and as an expression of love.

At Lourdes we learn to offer ourselves not only to divine justice but also—as St. Theresa of Lisieux* put it—to the merciful love of the one who, as I said in my Apostolic Letter *Salvifici Doloris,* suffered "voluntarily and innocently."

The Christian, like every other person of feeling and conscience, has a duty to work generously to bring about the alleviation of suffering, in order to obtain health—for himself or for others.

But his principal concern is to eliminate the most profound evil, sin. Vigorous physical health would be worthless if the soul were not at peace with God. If, however, the soul is in God's grace, even the most terrific pain will be made bearable, because the soul will understand its value for eternal health, our own and that of our brothers and sisters.

FEBRUARY 11, 1988

---

*St. Theresa of Lisieux (1873–97) was a Carmelite nun who wrote about her short life in "The Story of a Soul." Known as the Little Flower of Jesus, Thérèse Martin was canonized by Pope Pius XI in 1925 and was made a Doctor of the Church by John Paul II in 1997, only the third woman to be accorded this honor.

Why is it the sick who make pilgrimages to Lourdes? Why—we ask ourselves—has that place become for them a sort of "Cana in Galilee," to which they feel drawn in a special way? What attracts them to Lourdes with such force?

These people, if they are inspired by faith, turn to Lourdes. Why? Because they know that, as at Cana, "Jesus' Mother is there": and where she is so, too, is her Son. This is the certainty that drives the multitudes who every year pour into Lourdes in search of relief, of comfort, of hope. Sick people of every kind make the pilgrimage to Lourdes, sustained by the hope that, through Mary, the saving power of Christ may be manifested. And, in fact, that power is always revealed, by the gift of immense serenity and resignation; in some cases there is a general improvement in health, or even the grace of a complete cure, as numerous "instances" attest, which have been verified in the course of more than a hundred years.

However, the miraculous cure, in spite of everything, remains an exceptional event.

The saving power of Christ propitiated by the intercession of his mother is revealed at Lourdes *in the spiritual dimension above all*. It is in the hearts of the sick that Mary allows the thaumaturgical voice of her Son to be heard: a voice that generously melts the harsh iron core of bitterness and rebelliousness, and gives the soul eyes with which to see in a new light the world, and others, and our own destiny.

The sick discover at Lourdes the value of their own suffering. In the light of faith they are able to understand the fundamental meaning that suffering can have not only in their own life, inwardly renewed by that flame which consumes and transforms, but also in the life of the Church, the mystical body of Christ.

The Most Holy Virgin, who, standing courageously beside the Cross of her son on Calvary, shared in his Passion herself, can always persuade new souls to unite their sufferings to the sacrifice of Christ, in a choral "offering" that, bridging time and space, embraces all mankind and saves it.

February 11, 1980

"Blessed are you, Mary, among women!"

On the basis of this greeting of Elizabeth's, we, too, wish to raise to the Virgin a hymn of praise:

"Blessed are you among women and blessed is the fruit of your womb."

Blessed are you, O Mary, model of our faith and living image of our journey toward Christ.

Blessed are you, Virgin Mary, model of charity and maternal love for all those who seek consolation.

Blessed are you, who brought forth for us the source of life.

Blessed because you joined each one of us to the redeeming suffering of Christ Crucified, and called on us to serve those who suffer.

Blessed are you, because you precede us on the way of the Gospel and call on us to do what he, your Son, will tell us to do along the pathways of the world.

Blessed are you, because you teach us to love the poor, the humble, and the sinners, as God loves them.

Blessed are you, Mother of the Lord, and blessed is the fruit of your womb, Jesus Christ our Lord.

Amen!

February 11, 1992

Blessed is she who believed!

Blessed are those who live the word of the Lord!

Dearest brothers and sisters, open our hearts to the mystery of God's love,

direct our lives to the wealth of his forgiveness.

Thus we will have joy, we will have light, we will have life, for the divine mercy extends over those who fear it.

Forever.

> Mary, Immaculate Mother of God and men,
> hear the prayers of the sick,
> listen to our invocations,
> give peace to the world, Jesus,
> our true peace.
> Amen!

FEBRUARY 11, 1991

Do Not Forget the Sick

Feel useful to the world and the Church

Dear sick people, I would like to express my respect and affectionate concern for you. In the midst of your sufferings, whether physical or moral, and your doubts and hopes, may you be able to overcome the feeling of uselessness that sometimes grips you. May you find in the friendship of your brothers and sisters, neighbors, and friends, or in faith in Christ, the strength to endure all the "why"s that rise from your heart and the grace to feel yourselves useful to the world and to the Church.

SWITZERLAND,
JUNE 13, 1984

Blessed are you, you who suffer, you who, like Mary, believed in the fulfillment of the word of the Lord! May your faith always be solid and secure, founded on the rock of God's word! In fact you have a privileged place in Providence's design for salvation and so in the very structure of the Church, the mystical body of Christ. You have an importance and a real, if invisible and mysterious, influence on the unfolding of history and in the development of the mission of the Church. May the warmest feelings of gratitude on the part of the entire ecclesial community come to you who suffer, and to those who love you and help you.

FEBRUARY 11, 1987

Each of you, dear sick people, is called to be an apostle for mankind today. From the height of his Cross, Jesus says to each of those who suffer physically or morally:

— Remember that your suffering is evangelizing, because amid the travails of a society distracted and conditioned by a thousand earthly interests, you keep alive the supreme question of the meaning of life, you remind us of the realities that transcend time and history, you goad us to charity and love, you urge us to prayer and invocation!

— Remember that your suffering is sanctifying, because it purifies feelings, transforms impulses and passions, detaches us from the transient goods of the world, elevates us to the contemplation of our eternal destiny, leads us to reflect on the fundamental values of Revelation and Redemption, inspires us to appreciate "sanctifying grace," lets us taste the immense joy of the Eucharistic presence of Christ, calms us with the thought of the Paradise that awaits us. In fact, as St. Peter wrote, "if when you do right and suffer for it you take it patiently, you have God's approval. For to this you have been called, because Christ also suffered for you, leaving you an example, that you should follow in his steps."

— Remember, finally, that your suffering is redeeming, because those who suffer in union with Christ not only gain from him the strength necessary to accept it but complete with their suffering what is lacking in Christ's afflictions, according to the consoling assurance of St. Paul. As I wrote in the Apostolic Letter *Salvifici Doloris,* "In bringing about the Redemption through suffering, Christ has also raised human suffering to the level of the Redemption. Thus each man, in his suffering, can also become a sharer in the redemptive suffering of Christ." The world needs the Truth that Christ revealed; the world needs the salvation that Christ brought: there is no truth and no eternal salvation outside of him! And redemption is brought about also through the Calvary of your suffering!

MAY 23, 1987

and the Priests. Help the Church and the world with your prayers and with the trusting acceptance of your burden and your trials.

In the same way, let us pray for you and so help you to bear your fate with patience and faith.

GERMANY,
MAY 1, 1987

We all await the Resurrection

Now I would like to remain silent.

I would like to do only one thing: silently take your hand in mine to show you that I am among you, that I share your sufferings and your worries. In this sense I wish to comfort and encourage you.

But I would also like to talk to you. We are deeply bound by our common faith in Jesus Christ, who suffered and was resurrected from death. Through suffering and death Christ arrived at the Resurrection. We all share this Christian hope. We who are still living, those who are sick and suffering, old people who are aware that the hour of departure is ever closer. And, in their tombs, the dead, too, who went to sleep with this hope.

We all await resurrection.

With this perspective of faith we can live, we can even bear patiently the burden of our suffering, and we can die trustingly, since we have the assurance: "In you, O Lord, I have placed my hope, I will not be lost for eternity." Dear brothers and sisters, who are old and suffering.

Know that the Church needs you in a special way. The Pope, too, needs you.

We all need your prayers and the wise counsel of your age. We need the sacrifice of your sufferings for the Church and the world.

Thus, you can do much more for the renewal of the Church and the peace of the world than those who are healthy, and able to work. Help the Pope, your Bishop,

Do not forget the sick and the old.
Do not abandon the handicapped
and the gravely ill.
Do not relegate them to the margins of society.
Because if you do so,
you ignore the fact that they embody an impor-
    tant truth.

The sick, the old,
the handicapped, and the infirm
teach us that weakness
is a creative part of human life
and that suffering can be accepted
without loss of dignity.

In the absence of these persons among you,
you might be tempted
to think of physical health,
of force and power
as the only important values
to achieve in life.

But the wisdom of Christ
and the power of Christ
are visible in the weakness
of those who share his sufferings.

Let us place the sick and the handicapped
at the center of our life.
Let us protect them
and gratefully acknowledge
the debt that we owe them.

When we think of giving them something,
we will end up by realizing
that we are indebted to them.

May God bless and comfort
all those who suffer. And may Jesus Christ,
the Savior of the world
and healer of the sick,
make his light shine
through human weakness
as a guide for us
and for all humanity.
Amen.

ENGLAND,
MAY 28, 1982

Arise

How many times and on how many occasions do men
need this invitation repeated to them?

ARISE

You who are disappointed,

ARISE

You who have no more hope,

ARISE

You who are used to misery and no longer believe that
one can build something new.

ARISE

because God is about to make "all things new."

ARISE

You who are inured to God's gifts

ARISE

You who have lost the capacity to wonder

ARISE

You who have lost the confidence to call God "father"

ARISE

and regain your admiration for God's goodness.

ARISE

You who suffer

ARISE

You to whom life seems to have denied much

ARISE

while you feel excluded, abandoned, marginalized:

ARISE

because Christ has shown you his love and reserves for
you an unhoped-for possibility of fulfillment.

ARISE

JUNE 8, 1986

Special thanks to Stanley Browne, Martin Schmukler, Esq., and Marvin Kaplan of Marstan Associates, Ltd. Thanks also to the Libreria Editrice Rogate (LER), Father Nunzio Spinelli, and the Very Reverend Father Leonardo Sapienza, respectively, for the publication and the compilation of the anthologies. And to Rick Garson, Enzo Zullo, Alan R. Kershaw, Advocate of the Apostolic Tribunal of the Roman Rota, Paul Schindler, Esq., Larry Shire, Esq., Gil Karson, Esq., of Grubman, Indursky and Schindler.

KAROL WOJTYLA, POPE JOHN PAUL II, was born in Wadowice, in Poland, in 1920. He studied literature and drama in Kraków and later worked at a stone quarry and at a chemical plant. During the German occupation of Poland in World War II, he began preparing for the priesthood and was ordained in 1946. Wojtyla became bishop of Kraków in 1958, archbishop in 1964, and cardinal in 1967. He was elected Pope in 1978 and is the 264th Bishop of Rome.

you accept the sufferings that are inflicted on you, your prayer and your sacrifice to God will have an incredible force. Therefore pray at all times!

Pray and sacrifice for the Church and for the salvation of men, and also pray for my apostolic mission.

AUSTRIA,
JUNE 26, 1988

With its participation in suffering the Church becomes the dwelling place of God

Dear brothers and sisters! Of course there are always people who will carelessly and indifferently pass by you. They will make you feel insignificant and useless. But you may be sure that *we need you!* All society needs you. You continually question your neighbors about the profound meaning of human existence. You stimulate their solidarity, test their capacity to love. Above all, you challenge young people to give the best of themselves.

You inspire them to solidarity and willingness to help those who have a greater need for help. Where this solidarity is stifled, society is deprived of human warmth. Yet it is encouraging to see that many young people today are committed to serving the old, the sick, and the handicapped.

While I am with you, I wish to address all society: there should be no discrimination with regard to the value of human life. This discrimination gave rise, some decades ago, to one of the worst barbarities. There are not some lives that have value and others that do not. Every human life both before and after birth, whether it has fulfilled its potential or is handicapped—every human life has received its dignity from God, and no one can violate it. Every man is made in the image of God!

In conclusion I wish to repeat again that the Church needs you. *In you we recognize the presence of Christ who continues to live among us marked by the Cross and by suffering.* And if